MW01233866

The Divina Commedia And Canzoniere

Henry Holiday

DANTE AND BEATRICE

[illegible]

[illegible]

[illegible]

IN FIVE VOLUMES

BOSTON, U.S.A.
D. C. HEATH & CO., PUBLISHERS
1899

DANTE

THE DIVINA COMMEDIA AND CANZONIERE

Translated by the late

E. H. PLUMPTRE D.D.

Dean of Wells

WITH NOTES, STUDIES AND ESTIMATES

IN FIVE VOLUMES

BOSTON, U.S.A.

D. C. HEATH & CO., PUBLISHERS

1899

DANTE

VOL IV CANZONIERE

CONTENTS

CANZONIERE

CONTENTS

CONTENTS

CONTENTS

CANZONIERE

SONNET I

THE FIRST VISION OF LOVE

A ciascun' alma presa, e gentil core

To each enamoured soul, each gentle heart,
Within whose ken comes what I now indite,
That they their thoughts on what it means
may write,
Greeting in Love, their Lord, I now impart.

SONNET I

For us this Sonnet has the interest of being the earliest of Dante's extant writings. It is obvious, however, that it is not the work of a prentice-hand, and that though he was only eighteen, there may well have been some four or five years' study and practice, first of Latin, then of Provençal, and then of Italian poetry. The story is told in the *V. N.* (c. 3). Nine years after Beatrice had inspired his precocious boyhood with a consuming passion (1284), during which he had only had casual glimpses of her, probably in the Church of S. Lucia, he had met her, accompanied by two older friends, after her marriage with Simon de' Bardi, in the street, and she had for the first time given him a friendly greeting with words as well as looks. As a married woman, she was free to grant him a recognition which would before have been unmaidenly. The old flame, which perhaps had slumbered after he had heard of her marriage, was rekindled, and he went home to dream what is here recorded. As told in the Sonnet, still more as told in the *V. N.*, it is noteworthy as being the only instance of any approach to the sensuous element of passion. To see what Dante says he saw indicates a perilous, though involuntary, nearness to temptation. Even here, however, the corrective is near at hand. Joy is turned to mourning. The sleep of the beloved one, even then, is as the shadow-sister of death. After the manner of the time, perhaps with some exultation in the consciousness of a new-born power, Dante sent his poem to

Night's hours were minished just by one-third
part, 5
What time when every star shows brightest
sheen,
When all at once Love by mine eyes was seen,
Whose very memory makes my spirit start.
Joyous seemed Love, and he my heart did press
Within his hands, and in his arms he bare 10
My lady, sleeping, wrapt in silken sheet;
Then woke her, and that burning heart to eat,
Gave her; she fed with timid, lowly air.
Then as he went, tears did his grief confess.

his friends, among them to Guido Cavalcanti, Cino da Pistoia, Dante da Maiano. Of these, none understood the drift of what in later years he felt had been an unconscious prophecy of Beatrice's early death. Cavalcanti saw in it an instance of the melancholy that mingles with the sweet dreams of love. Cino suggested that Love came to bring him that which his heart desired, and then wept for the sorrow which his passion would bring to Beatrice. His namesake, more cynically, hinted that he was "off his head" and had better consult a doctor.

5 Four hours of the night had passed, *sc.*, it was between 1 and 2 A.M., night beginning with Compline at 9 P.M. (*Purg.* ix. 8). Repeatedly Dante notes in the *Commedia* his belief that dreams after midnight come true, and then their meaning is seen (*H.* xxvi. 7; *Purg.* ix. 16–18, xix. 4).

8 Comp. *H.* i. 6, xxxii. 72, as instances of the same shuddering thrill of memory.

11 The word "Madonna" supplies the key to all that follows. In the recognised use of Italian poetry, as in the speech of common life, that term was applied to a married woman only (*Canz.* ii. 13; *Witte, L. G.* ii. 19). The maiden was a *donzella* or *pulzella* (comp. a Sonnet by Frescobaldi, in which he elaborately discusses the advantages of loving one or the other, in Bart. *Lett. Ital.* iv. p. 17). The title thus given proves Beatrice's marriage at the commencement of the *V. N.* beyond the shadow of doubt. What Dante tells us in the *V. N.* (c. 6), that he wrote a *serventese* on the sixty fairest ladies of Florence, leads to the same conclusion. It would have been a breach of conventional etiquette to have inserted a maiden's name in such a poem. A. Pucci, in a poem of the same kind, names twenty-two ladies, and in each case has a word of praise for the husband also (*Lubin.* p. 19). If that conclusion seems at first startling, we may remember that it was the familiar practice of Provençal poets to choose a married woman as the object of a homage in which, ideally at least, there was no element of sensuous desire, only the supreme reverence for grace, beauty, purity. It was, we may admit, a strained relation, not without its risks, and too often the "vaulting ambition" might

SONNET II

WHAT MIGHT HAVE BEEN

Guido, vorrei che tu e Lapo ed io

GUIDO, I would that Lapo, thou, and I
Were taken by some skilled enchanter's spell,
And placed on board a barque that should
speed well

"o'erleap itself" and "fall o' the other side;" but, as the sequel shows, it was for Dante not a *liaison dangereuse*, but a purifying pain. His love was like that of Sordello, not for Cunizza, but for another Beatrice, the wife of Charles of Anjou (*Purg.* vi. 58 *n.*), purer than that of Petrarch for his Laura, also a "*donna*," the wife of Hugh de Sade. In the Sonnet before us, the first that he cared to leave to future ages, he was perhaps following in Sordello's footsteps, and in those of Guido Guinicelli, whom he recognised as his master (*Purg.* xxvi. 98), claiming for himself, however, the distinctive merit of rising out of the traditional conventionalities of the Troubadours and other poets, and writing as love taught him (*Purg.* xxiv. 52–54).

12 The meaning of the vision is not far to seek. His heart burned with a reverential love, which Beatrice accepted, not as another woman might have done, triumphant in a new conquest, but with a timid meekness; and Love wept at the coming sorrow, in which, as a strange foreboding indicated, the homage was to end.

SONNET II

Notable as the one Sonnet in which the element of a sportive joy, what Quinet has called "the aureole of adolescence," is dominant. How bright and happy might life be, it seems to say, could we but live in an enchanted region, where its stern realities (among them Beatrice's marriage) had no place. It is suggestive that he did not think fit to include it in the *V. N.*

1 The Guido is Cavalcanti, then Dante's chiefest friend, before his change of feeling as to Virgil's merits or the Epicurean materialism which he inherited from his father had brought about the coolness and alienation which *H.* x. 52–63 *n.* at least suggests.

Through wind and wave, and with our will
comply;
So that nor evil chance nor stormy sky 5
Should be to our desire impediment.
So, living always in one full consent,
Desire should grow to dwell in company:
And Lady Vanna, Lady Bicè too,
With her who nobly fills my thirtieth
line— 10
Would that the good enchanter these might
move
With us to speak for evermore of Love;
And each of them in full content combine,
E'en as I deem 'twould be with me and you!

[9] Vanna, or Giovanna, known also as Primavera (=Spring), and mentioned again in *V. N.* c. 24, *S.* 16, was the object of Cavalcanti's love. Bice, as in her father's will (*Frat. V. D.* p. 98), stands for Beatrice. The third is described as thirtieth in the list of sixty fair ones of Florence, on whom Dante had written a poem of the *serventese* type (see *n.* on *S.* 1), which has not come down to us, and in which Beatrice's name appeared, as by the decree of fate, as the *ninth*. She has been identified with the Donna (the beloved one, not the wife) of Lapo Gianni, or, as some say, Lapo degli Uberti, the son of Farinata, and father of the poet Fazio, who wrote the *Dittamondo*, a kind of Gazetteer in *terza rima*. The fact that Guido Cavalcanti married the daughter of the Farinata of *H.* x. 32 is in favour of the latter view, as also is the mention of Lapo in *V. E.* i. 13. There also he is grouped with Cavalcanti, probably with Dante himself. The leading thought of the Sonnet is the wish that the ideal love could become a life-long reality. But he knows it cannot be. Only the enchanter's wand could bring about such a transformation. The actual history of what was then future presents one of the strange contrasts which so often characterise the "irony of history." Beatrice died in 1290. Cavalcanti was banished by Dante to Sarrazzano, and died of a fever caught in its unwholesome climate in 1300. For Dante himself there was a life of poverty and exile. It may be noted that in some MSS. "Lagia" takes the place of "Bice," as though the Sonnet had been written by Cino of Pistoia, who addresses many of his poems to a Selvaggia, a name of which Lagia may have been a diminutive.

CANZONIERE

BALLATA I

"DE PROFUNDIS"

O voi, che per la via d' Amor passate

O YE who on Love's path pursue your way,
Behold and say
If there be any sorrow grave as mine:
That ye would list to me is all I pray,
And then let Fancy's play
Judge if of all woe I am key and shrine. 6

Love, not for little good that in me lay,
But his own noble goodness to display,

BALLATA I

The *V. N* (c. 7) gives the following account of the poem, which is there called a Sonnet, that term being used, at first, in a less restricted sense than it acquired afterwards. This particular form was known as a *Sonetto doppio* or *rinterzato*. Dante had sought to conceal his love, but he could not refrain from gazing on Beatrice as he knelt in church, probably in that of S. Lucia, in the *Via de' Bardi*, and near her husband's house. In so gazing, another fair lady sat between him and his beloved one, and many thought, therefore, that he was in love with her. The poet saw in that mistake a means at once of concealment and of utterance. He would encourage it by writing poems which should seem to be addressed to her, and yet give vent to thoughts that were meant for Beatrice. She was to be, as he says, his "screen" against whispering tongues and over-curious gaze. And this went on, he says, for some months, and even years. It was in connection with this phase of his passion that he wrote the *Serventese* above referred to. Her departure from Florence gave him an opportunity for pouring forth his sorrow as though that had been its cause. For the history of the *Serventese*, see Diez, *Troub.*, pp. 169–176.

2 The allusion to *Lam.* i. 1 finds a parallel in Dante's quotations from the same prophet in his Epistle to the Cardinals (*Ep.* 9). See also the note on *H.* i. 32, and *V. N.* c. 29, 31.

Placed me in life so pleasant and so fair,
That oft I heard behind me voices say, 10
"Ah, through what merit may
His heart so light be, and so free from care?"
Now have I all my wonted courage lost,
Which came of old from Love's great treasure-store,
Whence I continue poor, 15
And shrink when I would any one accost.

And thus, desiring still to act like those,
Who, in their shame, hide their deficiencies,
Cheerful I meet men's eyes,
And weep within and wail o'er all my woes. 20

SONNET III

DEATH OF BEATRICE'S FRIEND (I)

Piangete, amanti, poichè piange Amore

WEEP, all ye lovers, seeing Love doth weep,
Hearing what cause calls forth his piteous cry:
Love hears fair ladies mourn in sympathy,

[13] The change is like that of *S.* i. 9–14. The first joy of the new passion, the dream of the impossible, as in *S.* ii. had turned into a consuming sorrow.

[17] We note the characteristically subjective self-analysis, the forerunner of many like it in the *Commedia* (*H.* i. 6, xxxii. 72; *Purg.* v. 20, vii. 10, xxx. 74–79, xxxi. 64–66; *Par.* vii. 10), the same proud reticence and reserve which characterised the poet from first to last.

SONNET III

Early in the history of the *V. N.* (c. 8)—probably before 1285—one of Beatrice's best-loved friends died, in the full freshness of her

Whose eyes give outward proof of sorrow deep.
For villainous Death on gentle heart doth heap 5
The strokes of his most cruel workmanship,
Wasting what winneth praise from each man's lip,
In lady fair, save th' honour she doth keep.
Hear ye what homage Love to her did pay:
For I saw him lament in very deed, 10
Over the lifeless form he came to view:
And often to high heaven his glance he threw,
Where finds a home the gentle spirit freed,
Who was a lady of such presence gay.

youth, and Dante laments her death in this and the following poem. He describes her as in some respects the complement of Beatrice. She is gay, bright, full of a ready courtesy. God had taken her to Himself, and she was in the courts of Heaven. I have ventured (*Purg.* xxviii. 40 *n.*), on what seem to me sufficient grounds, to identify her with the Matilda of the Earthly Paradise. In Dante's admiration and reverence she clearly occupied a place second only to Beatrice.

10 The Love who mourns is not the classical Cupid, but Beatrice herself—Love incarnate, whom Dante had seen weeping over the body of her friend (*V. N.* c. 8). That upward look implied the prayer that they might meet again. In the *Purgatory* vision Dante implies his belief that the prayer had been granted, though the transfigured Beatrice dwelt in the higher region of the Empyrean heaven, Matilda in the Earthly Paradise—the one symbolising the wisdom of the contemplative life, the other the joy of active ministration.

BALLATA II

DEATH OF BEATRICE'S FRIEND (2)

Morte villana, di pietà nemica

O VILLAIN Death, of pity ruthless foe,
Old parent of great woe,
Inevitable doom and hard to bear,
Since thou hast filled my heart with sad despair,
And to and fro I wander full of care, 5
My tongue in blaming thee doth weary grow;

And if I seek thee pitiless to show,
Needs must I make men know
Thy guilt, wherein all wrongs most wrongful are.
Not that 'tis hidden from men's eyes afar, 10
But to rouse all to fiery heat of war,
Who henceforth shall with Love's true nurture grow.

Thou from the world hast ta'en all courtesy,
And virtue, that which wins a lady praise:
In youth's first gladsome days 15
Thou hast laid low all Love's sweet pleasantry.

BALLATA II

From *V. N.* c. 8, and a variation of the theme of *S.* iii.

More I tell not who that fair dame may be,
Than by the exceeding grace each act displays.
Who treads not life's true ways,
Let him not hope to have her company. 20

SONNET IV

LOVE AS PILGRIM

Cavalcando l' altr' ier per un cammino

RIDING the other day along a road,
All pensive o'er the thought that made me sad,
I found Love half-way on my journey, clad
In the light garb that pilgrim's raiment showed.
Like one of low estate he on did plod, 5
As though his lordship he had cast aside,
And sighing, full of thought, his course he plied,
That he might look on none, with head low bowed.

17–20 Grammatically the lines can only refer to the friend of Beatrice, for whom Dante mourns; but he assures us in the *V. N.* that they were meant for Beatrice herself. Possibly the lines were written at first for Matilda, found to be fitter for Beatrice, and so mentally transferred to her. It must be remembered that he had already in *S.* iii. identified Love with Beatrice.

SONNET IV

From *V. N.* c. 9, where also we are told of the vision which it embodies, and which came to him when he was riding with many others along a rushing stream. I surmise, with Witte, Krafft, Wegele (p. 74), that it connects itself with the expedition against Arezzo, in which Dante took part (1289), and which ended in the

When he saw me he called me by my name,
And said, "I come from region distant far, 10
Where through my will, thy heart had ta'en its flight.
And now I bring it for a new delight,"
Such measure full of him I then did share,
He fled, nor saw I how he went and came.

SONNET V

SEPARATION

Se'l bello aspetto non mi fosse tolto

Were the sweet sight from me not ta'en away
Of that fair lady whom I long to see,
For whom I sigh and weep in misery,
Thus distant from her face so blithe and gay,

battle of Campaldino (*H.* xxii. 6; *Purg.* v. 92), and that the stream was the Arno, and I find in it the expression of a new-born sense of freedom rising out of the activities of that stirring life. He is no longer under the despotism of Love; his heart no longer devoured by her to whom Love has given it. As he rides he sees Love as a pilgrim (probably enough an actual pilgrim met the cavaliers on their way), with that peculiarly humble look which devout pilgrims affect, and that seems to him the symbol of the state to which what had been the master-passion of his soul is now reduced. The absorption of the mind by one engrossing thought, the waking vision even while he is riding with a troop of horse, is eminently characteristic of the seer-temperament (*Purg.* xv. 115, *n.*). He is not far from the home of her who had screened his love, but love gives him leave to turn his heart to any new delight, whether it be that of battle or the beauty of some new fair one, to be in the future what the "screen" lady had been in the past.

SONNET V

Not in the *V. N.*, but belonging probably to the same period as

That, which as heavy load on me doth weigh, [8]
  And makes me feel such torment keen and
      dire,
  After such fashion, that I half expire,
Like one with whom his hope no more will stay,
Would be but light, and with no terror dread;
  But since no more I see her as of old, [10]
  Love pains me, and my heart with grief is
      cold.
And so of every comfort I lose hold,
  That all things which delight on others shed
  To me are troublous, and work woe instead.

CANZONE I

THE LOVER'S PLEA FOR PITY

La dispietata mente che pur mira

My sorrowing soul that only looks behind
  On days gone by of which I now am reft,
  On this side with my heart holds conflict sore;

S. iv., distance from the object of love being the link that connects the two. Here, however, the sense of freedom has passed away. The pains of absence are more keenly felt, the lover misses the daily glance, the occasional salutation, which have been the light of his life. Such may well have been the state of Dante's soul during the Campaldino or Caprona expedition. Fraticelli, however, conjectures that the absence complained of may be that caused by the death of Beatrice, while Balbo assumes that the journey was one to Bologna in company with other students. We owe the discovery of the Sonnet to Witte's researches in the Ambrosian Library at Milan.

CANZONE I

Not in the *V. N.*, but connected by the fact of distance from

On that, fond longing that calls back my
mind
To the sweet country that I now have left, 5
With the strong might of Love prevaileth
more.
Nor feel I now within the strength of yore
That can for long ward off my sore defeat,
Unless, that help, dear Lady, comes from
thee,
Wherefore, if thine it be 10
To set it free by vigorous emprise meet,
May it please thee to send thy greeting
dear,
To bid its virtue be of better cheer.

May it please thee, my Lady, yet again,
Thou fail not now the heart that loves thee
so, 15
Since from thee only succour it can claim.
A good knight never rides with tightened
rein,
To help a squire who calls him in his woe;
For not for him alone he fights, but fame.
And sure its grief now burns with fiercer
flame, 20

Florence (l. 5) in Beatrice's lifetime, with the two preceding Sonnets.

In *St.* i. we have the story of an inner conflict. There is the sorrow of remembering happier days, which lie behind him in the distance (*H.* v. 122); there is the desire, though duty calls elsewhere, to go back to the scene of those days. Will not his beloved help him to find peace by sending him, written or orally, the salutation which when spoken had filled his soul with such rapturous delight (*V. N.* c. 3, 9, 10, 18), which made *saluto* and *salute* interchangeable terms?

17-19 Few great poets delight more than Dante does in bringing out the nobleness of the true relation of master and servant, knight and squire. The three lines breathe the very spirit of an ideal chivalry by which the young soldier was, we may believe, inspired in his first campaign. *H.* xvii. 90; *Par.* xxiv. 148.

When, I think, O my Lady fair, that thou
Art painted in it by the hands of Love;
So should'st thou much more prove
For him thy care in greater measure now,
Since He, from whom all good must needs appear, 25
For His own image in us holds us dear.

If thou would'st speak, thou Hope, of all most sweet,
Of more delay of that which I request,
Know thou I cannot any longer wait,
For all my strength to bear doth waning fleet; 30
And this 'tis fit thou know, since my unrest
Moves me to seek my last hope ere too late:
For man should bear with patience every weight
Till the last burden which to death must press,
Before he seek his greatest friend to prove, 35
Not knowing what his love:
And if it chance he heed not my distress
Then is there nothing that can cost more dear,
For death has nought more rapid or more drear.

22-26 The passage has often been misinterpreted, but its meaning is sufficiently clear. God, from whom all goodness flows, holds us dear because He sees in us His own image; so should Beatrice have pity on her lover, for Love has painted her form on the canvas of his soul. The thought is eminently characteristic of the poet, who, even then, was also a theologian.

33 Another touch of the nobleness of chivalry. The young soldier of Campaldino has learnt that he must not call for help, however ready his friend may be to give it (l. 17), except under the strongest pressure of necessity. That he appeals to Beatrice now (the poem is obviously addressed to her), is a proof that he has reached that point.

And thou alone art she whom most I love, 40
Who upon me canst greatest gift bestow,
In whom alone my hope finds fullest rest:
Only to serve thee would I long life prove.
And those things, whence to thee may honour flow,
I seek and crave; all else doth me molest; 45
Where others fail, thou canst grant all my quest.
For Yes and No entirely in thy hand
Hath Love now left; whence I esteem me great:
The trust thou dost create
Springs from thy bearing, pitiful and bland; 50
For whoso looks on thee in truth knows well
From fair outside that there doth mercy dwell.

Now, therefore, let thy greeting quickly speed,
And come within the heart that waits for it,
My gentle Lady;—thou my prayer hast known. 55
But know, the entrance there is barred indeed
With that same arrow wherewith I was hit,
Which Love shot when he made me all his own:
By it the way is closed to every one,
Save to Love's envoys, who to ope have skill, 60
By will of that same Power that doth it bar:
Wherefore, in this my war,
Its coming would to me be grievous ill,

43-45 Evidence, if that were needed, of the purity of the poet's passion. All that he craves for is the opportunity of serving his beloved and doing honour to her name, and that service is its own exceeding great reward.

55-65 One notes the recurrence of military imagery, the arrow used as a bolt, the closed gate of the fortress, the arrows of love's artillery,

If it approach without the company
Of that Lord's envoys, who imprisons me. [65]

Canzon', thy journey should be swift and short,
For well thou know'st how brief is now the
day
For him for whom thou speedest on thy way.

BALLATA III

EYES DIM WITH SORROW

In abito di saggia messagera

In fashion of an envoy wise and true,
Move on thine errand, Song, without delay,
To my fair dame thy message to convey,
And tell her my life's powers are faint and
few.

such as may have been suggested by the siege of Caprona, the warfare by which the soul's peace is imperilled.

[66] After the manner of the Provençal poets, the Canzone terminates with what was known as the *Tornato* or *L'Envoi* of the poem, considered as a messenger who has to bear tidings to her to whom it is sent. The last two lines seem to indicate something like an anticipation, which the state of Dante's health, as described in *V. N.* c. 14, 23, might well warrant, of an early death. The time was short; Beatrice would do well to give a proof of her sympathy before it was too late. See *B.* iii.

BALLATA III

The whole poem connects itself closely with the last lines of the foregoing. In the "wreath of torturing fire" by which his eyes were encirled (l. 10) we have the poet's version of the weakness of sight described in *S.* xxix.; *C.* xl.; *Conv.* iii. 9; and in *V. N.*

Thou wilt begin to tell her that mine eyes, 5
Through looking on her angel-countenance,
Were wont to bear the garland of desires.
Now, since they cannot see the face they prize,
Death with such terror on them doth advance,
That they have made a wreath of torturing fires. 10
Alas! I know not whither they should fare
For their delight, and so thou me wilt find
As one half-dead, unless thou bring my mind
Comfort from her; therefore tell her my prayer.

BALLATA IV

"APOLOGIA PRO VITÂ SUÂ"

Ballata, io vo' che tu ritruovi Amore

I WILL that thou, my Song, find Love anew,
And that with him thou seek my lady fair,
So that my pleading, with thy sweet-voiced air,
My Lord to her may speak in accents true.

c. 11, 12. They, in their mute suffering, are even without words, as an appeal *ad misericordiam*. Not in the *V. N.*, but probably one of the poems referred to in *C.* v. as addressed to the "screen" lady.

BALLATA IV

From *V. N* c. 12 The contrivance of the "screen," who was to serve as a lay-figure of the true object of the poet's love, had led, as

Thou goest, my Song, so full of courtesy, 5
That, though no friend be near,
Thou oughtest to be bold on every side;
But if thou seekest full security,
First find if Love be there.
It is not good without him far to ride; 10
For she to whom thou should'st thy tale confide,
If, as I deem, she is with me irate,
And thou shouldst go without him as thy mate,
Might lightly on thee some dishonour do.

With a sweet sound, when with him thou shalt be, 15
Do thou these words begin,
As soon as thou her pity shalt have sued:
"My Lady, he who sends me now to thee,
Seeks, if thy will he win,
That thou should'st hear if his defence be good. 20
'Tis Love who makes him, as may suit his mood,

might have been expected, in the case of the second lady who was selected for this purpose, to misunderstandings. Beatrice was indignant at what appeared to her his fickleness, a fickleness which brought some scandal on the lady's reputation, and he writes by way of explanation, with a plea of "not guilty." He may have seemed faithless, but his heart has all along been true. Love, indeed, has told him in a vision that it is time that these screens and counterfeits should cease. All that he seeks is to serve Beatrice whether in life, or should she so will it, in his death (ll. 25-34). We note that the poem was to be set to music, "*Di soave armonia.*" A friend (H. W. P.) notes the coincidence of thought in Herrick's poem to Anthea—

"Bid me to live, and I will live;
. . . .
Bid me despair; . . .
Or bid me die, and I will dare
E'en death to die for thee."

Change look and hue for your fair beauty's
sake:
Bethink thee, then, why he his eye doth make
On others look, though heart unchanged be
true."

Tell her, "O Lady, still his heart hath borne 25
Such firm unwavering faith,
That every thought prompts him to service
due;
Quick was he thine, nor ever thence was
torn."
If she doubt what he saith,
Bid her of Love demand if it be true; 30
And at the end with meek entreaty sue
To pardon him, if he hath caused her pain;
And if she bid me die by message plain,
Her slave that hest obeying she shall view.

And say to him who holds all pity's key, 35
Before thou leave my fair,
He put forth skill on my good plea to dwell,
Through grace of my sweet-flowing melody.
* Remain thou with her there,
And of thy servant what thou willest, tell; 40
And if thy prayer her pardon winneth well,
Bid her with aspect fair to speak of peace."
O gentle song of mine, if thee it please,
Speed at such time that honour may accrue.

42 The closing prayer is for a message of greeting (*salute* in its twofold sense), such as had been asked for in *Canz.* i.

SONNET VI

INNER CONFLICT

Tutti li miei pensier parlan d'amore

My every thought is fain to speak of love,
  And in them there is such variety,
  That one constrains me own his sovereignty,
Another will his power a madness prove;
A third, by giving hope, sweet joy doth move, 5
  And many a time and oft one bids me cry;
  Only in craving pity come they nigh
Accord, and with heart-tremblings sadly rove.
Whence I know not to what point I should
    wend,
  And wish to speak, yet know not what to
    say: 10
  So find myself in amorous wanderings lost.
And if I would agree with all the host,
  I must needs now to her my fair foe pray,
  That she, my Lady Pity, me defend.

SONNET VI

From *V. N.* c. 13. An expansion of the inner conflict of emotions indicated in *Canz.* i. l. 62. All however agree, and this is their point of contact with *Ball.* iii. in their prayer for pity. Is love good or not good? Does the sweetness of the word "*Amore*" correspond with the reality, on the principle that *Nomina sunt consequentia rerum?* In applying the name "Madonna" to the "pity" which he seeks, there is, he says in the *V. N.*, a touch of irony. Pity is not the mistress of his soul.

SONNET VII

TRANSFORMATION

Coll' altre donne mia vista gabbate

WITH other dames thou dost my looks deride,
And think'st not, Lady, what hath wrought the change,
That makes me wear a face so new and strange,
When on thy beauteous form mine eyes abide.
Did'st thou but know it, Pity had denied 5
Longer to prove me with the old distress,
For Love, whene'er he sees me near thee press,
Puts on such boldness and such sturdy pride,

SONNET VII

The history is given in *V. N.* c. 14. The poet, returned to Florence, had been at a wedding-feast, where there were many guests. Suddenly Beatrice appeared among them. In part, perhaps, through the confusion and shame implied in *Ball.* iii. and iv., he turned giddy, leant against the wall to save himself from falling, and had to be led back to his own house. As he goes out he hears the ladies who were present, Beatrice among them (only married ladies attended such gatherings, they were all *donne*, *S.* i. *n.*), talk of him, not without a tone of derision, and when he comes to himself in the "chamber of tears," he writes by way of protest against her hastiness. He had not yet learnt the lesson, "Let the people talk." (*Purg.* v. 13.)

Many commentators infer that the marriage-feast was that of Beatrice's own wedding, and that this was the cause of Dante's overpowering emotion. For the reasons given in the notes on *S.* i., I am compelled to think otherwise. I surmise rather that it may have been the first time he had seen her since his return from Campaldino, and since the misunderstandings that had pained her (*Ball.* iv.). To look on her as sharing in a wedding-feast may well have renewed the feeling with which he had heard that she had been given to another, and had cursed the altered fashions of the time and the greed of gain which thus marred the happiness of his life (*Par.* xv. 103–105).

It smites my senses, making them afraid,
  Dooms this to death, and that to banish-
    ment, 10
  So that I stand alone to gaze on thee.
Wherefore another's look I take on me,
  Yet so that still I share the loud lament
  Of those the sufferers that are exiles made.

SONNET VIII

DRUNK, BUT NOT WITH WINE

Ciò, che m' incontra nella mente, more

THAT in my mind which clashes with it, dies,
  Whene'er I come to see thee, my fair Joy,
  And when I near thee stand, I hear Love's
    cries,
Who saith, "Flee far, if death brings thee
    annoy."

[9] I have translated *spiriti* by "senses," as the best equivalent. In Dante's physiology every sense, hearing, sight, &c., had its own special *spirito* (*V. N.* c. 1), but that meaning would not be conveyed to the reader by the English "spirits." Every such "sense" or "spirit" had been stunned as he gazed on Beatrice, and so the fashion of his countenance was altered and he became as another man, only so far retaining consciousness as to hear, as it were, the wailings of each banished sense. The concluding lines half suggest that those wailings seemed to him as an anticipation of the misery of the lost (*H.* iii. 25).

SONNET VIII

From *V. N.* c. 15. Obviously, in close connection with *Sonn.* vii., painting in verse what he had sketched before in prose. Why, he asked himself, should he seek to see her when the sight was so

My features paint my heart's hue in mine eyes,[8]
  Which, as in death-swoon, leans where rest
    is nigh,
  And drunken with great trembling and
    surprise,
It seems the stones cry out to me, "Die, die."
Who sees me then is guilty of a sin,
  Not comforting my soul, dismayed with ill, 10
  At least in proving that my woe doth gain
Some pity for me, whom your mirth doth kill,—
  That woe which shows itself in looks of pain
  In eyes which seek death of their own free
    will.

full of pain? And yet there rose up such a form of beauty in his mind that the desire to see her was stronger than ever. Would not Beatrice's mirth, that had so vexed his soul, be turned into pity when she read of it?

[8] We note the same reduplication in *Par.* viii. 75, and conjecture that the story of the Sicilian Vespers (1282) must have reached Florence within a few years of the date of the Sonnet, filling Dante's soul with horror, and transmuting itself into a symbol of the "soul's tragedy," through which he himself was passing. As before in *Ball.* iii., he pleads the special sufferings of his eyes to move his lady's pity.

SONNET IX

"NEC MORBOS, NEC REMEDIA PATI POSSUMUS"

Spesse fiate venemi alla mente

FULL many a time there comes into my thought
 The melancholy hue which Love doth give,
 And such woes come on me that I am
  brought
To say, "Ah me! doth one so burdened live?"
For Love with me so suddenly hath fought, 5
 That 'tis as though life all my frame did
  leave;
 One living spirit only help hath wrought,
And that remains discourse of thee to weave.
Then I arise, resolved myself to aid,
 And pale and wan, and of all strength bereft, 10
 I come to see thee, thinking health to find:
And if on thee my longing eyes are stayed,
 My heart, as with an earthquake, then is cleft,
 Which makes my pulse leave all its life
  behind.

SONNET IX

From *V. N.* c. 16. The conflict with the many "spirits" (in Dante's sense of the word) is continued. One only holds out, and that remains to tell the praises of the beloved one. Thus sore-smitten he looks to her in hope of healing, but alas! the remedy is worse than the disease (l. 11); fearfulness and trembling once more come on him.

CANZONE II

LAUDES BEATRICIS

Donne ch' avete intelletto d' amore

LADIES, who have intelligence of love,
I fain would of my Lady speak with you,
Not that I think to tell her praises due,
But speaking to set free my burdened soul.
I say that, as my thoughts on her worth
move, 5
So sweetly Love thrills all my senses through,
That if I lost not all my courage true
My words would make the world own Love's
control.

CANZONE II

V. N. c. 18 and 19. Memorable as probably the poem on which Dante looked as the masterpiece of his earlier works. It is the first *Canzone* which he inserts in the *V. N.* He quotes from it as his own in *V. E.* ii. 12, 13. In *Purg.* xxiv. 51, he makes Buonagiunta of Lucca, himself a poet, eager to know whether he meets the man who wrote it. His account of its genesis is that he was asked one day by many married and unmarried women of rank (*donne* and *donzelle*, not *femmine*) of Florence, when Beatrice was not with them, whose relations with their worshippers were quite other than those between him and Beatrice, what his love meant, what was to come of it all? And this is his reply. He who would enter into the mind and heart of Dante should read it line by line and word for word. He wished for nothing more than Beatrice's greeting. That was the only blessedness he sought for. And in saying this he was but repeating what Love itself had taught him. The form in which that thought was expressed came to him, he says, as he was walking by a clear river—probably the Arno.

1-14 The poet will not shrink from his task, though he feels that it lies far beyond his powers. Love is mighty though he is weak. Line 13 indicates the distinction between *donna* and *donzella*, already noted in *n.* on *Sonn.* i.

Such lofty strains I choose not for my rôle,
Lest I, through coward fear, should vile
become; 10
But of her gentle life I'll not be dumb,
And sketch with light touch that surpassing
whole,
Ladies and damsels who know Love, with
you;
For not to others now my speech is due.

An Angel speaketh in the Eternal Mind 15
And saith, "O Sire, in yonder world is shown
A wondrous thing, which hath to being grown
From a pure soul whose brightness shines on
high.
Heaven which no other sense of want doth
find
Than of her presence, asks of God that
boon; 20
And every saint implores for that alone."
And Pity only comes to help our fears,
For thus speaks God, who of my Lady hears,
"My well-beloved, now suffer ye in peace
That this your hope, as long as I shall please, 25
Wait, where one dwells whom loss of her
shall try,
And who shall tell the damned in hell's unrest
'I have beheld the hope of all the blest.'"

16 The lover has already taken a long stride towards the apotheosis of the *Commedia*. Beatrice is already as "God's true praise" (*H.* ii. 103). The saints in Paradise are waiting for her presence to complete their bliss. Pity only pleads that she may be left a little longer for her friends on earth.

28 One cannot read what follows without feeling that we have the first germ of the thought which afterwards, as in *V. N.* c. 23, ripened into a vision and then into a purpose (*V. N.* c. 43), and lastly into the wonder of wonders, the *Commedia* itself.

My Lady thus in highest heaven is sought:
Now will I ye her worth supreme should
hear. 30
I say, who will as gentle dame appear,
Let her go with her, for where she doth go,
In basest souls a chill by Love is wrought,
Freezing each vile thought till to death 'tis
near:
And who Love wills should see with vision
clear 35
Must either die or else must noble grow.
And when he finds one who doth worthy
show
To look on her, he doth her worth attest;
For that her greeting gives him peace and
rest,
So humbling him that he no wrath doth
know, 40
And, as yet greater grace, God gives her this;
He who speaks with her cannot end amiss.

Love saith of her, "A thing of mortal birth,
How can it be so beautiful and pure?"
Then he looks on her, inly swearing, "Sure 45
God means in her to work a wonder new."
Her hue is that of pearl of priceless worth,
Meet for a lady, fair without excess:
She is all good that Nature can express,
And in her, as a type, is beauty true. 50

36 Literature can hardly, I imagine, present a parallel to the nobleness of these lines. The holiness of a perfect and pure beauty freezes each thought of evil. Pride and desire alike are calmed. To have conversed with her is the source of unfailing hope. Here again we note the first germ of the *Commedia.* The natural development of that germ is seen in the thought that she herself must come to his rescue (as in *H.* ii. 103) in the "critical minute" of his life.

47 One of the few artist's touches in a portrait which otherwise is

From her fair eyes, when we their glances view,
Spirits pass forth inflamed with Love's sweet
blaze,
And strike the eyes of him who then doth
gaze,
And so pass on, each finds his heart anew.
Ye see them there, Love painted in her
smile, 55
Where fixèd gaze they may not brook long
while.

Canzon', I know that thou to many a fair
Wilt go discoursing, when I thee have sped.
Now do I warn thee, since I thee have bred
As Love's own daughter in her lowly prime, 60
That, where thou goest, thou utter still the
prayer,
"Teach me to journey, for to her I'm sent
Whose praises are my one chief ornament;"
And if, as weak and vain, thou fear'st to
climb:
Stay not where they dwell who are base with
crime: 65
Learn, if thou canst, to hold thy converse free
Only with man or maid of courtesy;
Who soon will speed thy way in quickest
time.

almost purely spiritual. In the "pearl on forehead white" of *Par.* iii. 14 we may well find a reminiscence of that touch. Comp. *Sonn.* xxvi.

52 The ever recurring theory of "spirits" comes in where modern poetry would speak of "influence" and "expression." The thrill that pervades the lover's frame when fair eyes look on him, whence can it come? So Dante asked, and made answer to himself, Where but from some occult forces, for which "spirits" was at least as good a term as any other (*V. N.* c. 2)? In l. 55 a *v. l.* gives *viso* ("face") for *riso*.

60 The *envoi* of the poem shows that it was meant to reach Beatrice herself, it may be as an atonement for the real or fancied

Thou wilt find Love with her, my Lady
sweet,
Commend me thou to them, as it is meet. 70

CANZONE III

RETROSPECTION

E'm' incresce di me sì malamente

So sad and keen a grief comes over me,
That full as much of pain,
Doth pity, as the grief itself, excite.
Ah me! for that, in saddest misery,
A power doth me constrain 5

neglect of the past (*Ball.* iv.). Dante hopes, however, for other readers, but is content that they should be "few," if only they be "fit." What he demands is the element, hard to be defined, of the "courtesy" which was so favourite a word with him (*H.* ii. 58, 134, iii. 121; *Purg.* ix. 92, xi. 85; *Par.* xii. 111), and was so eminently characteristic of his own nature.

CANZONE III

Not in the *V. N.*, but presenting so many points of contact with *C.* ii. that it well may be regarded as a sketch or an echo of it, and therefore as referring to Beatrice. Krafft, it is true, thinks that Dante speaks of the fair one whom he loved in the Casentino, but on grounds which seem to me quite inadequate; nor can I accept the view of another critic that it is addressed to the *donna gentile*, either as a flesh and blood reality, or as the symbol of philosophy (Oeynhausen). Yet one never feels quite sure that there may not be some allegoric or mystic meaning.

[3] The paradox rises probably out of the "screen" arrangement (*Ball.* iv.). Dante was pining for some token that Beatrice still cared for him, but the pity which his manifest distress called forth came from those who were not the objects of his love. The eyes which had given the hope of peace were now averted from him and

To pour my last sigh in a breathing light,
Within the heart which those fair eyes did smite,
When with his hands Love opened them to see,
To lead me to this season of my woe.
Ah me! how kind and free, 10
Pleasant and sweet, did they upon me rise,
When they, to my surprise,
Began to work the death which brings me low,
Saying, "Our light brings peace for thee to know:

Peace to thy heart we'll give, delight to thee." 15
So to these eyes of mine
Those of my Lady fair did sometimes say;
But when, with knowledge clear, they came to see
That through her power divine,
My spirit from me had nigh passed away, 20
They with Love's banners fled from out the fray,
So that their glorious and triumphant gleam
Was to mine eyes no longer visible:
And saddened still doth seem
My soul, which looked thence to be comforted, 25
And now, as though 'twere dead,
It sees the heart with which 'twas wed to dwell,
And it must part from that it loved so well.

left him desolate. He finds the meaning of a "sorrow's crown of sorrow" (*H.* v. 122).

Yea, loving well, it goeth wailing sore,
From out this life's confine, 30
Disconsolate, for Love doth banish her.
She travels hence, so sorrowing more and more,
That, ere she pass the line,
Her Maker listens and doth pitying hear.
Within the heart, pent up in inmost sphere, 35
With what life yet remains all weak and spent,
In that respect that she hath passed away,
There she pours her lament
For Love who drives her from the world to flee;
And oft with them would be, 40
The spirits, which go sorrowing alway,
Because their help-mate doth no longer stay.

The image of this Lady fair doth dwell
Yet in my mind so clear,
Where Love hath placed it, he who was her guide; 45
Nor doth the ill she sees upon her tell:
So is she now more fair
Than ever, with a smile beatified:
And eyes that work my death she opens wide,
And wails o'er her who doth her going weep. 50
"Go, wretched soul, thy way; yea, rise and go,"
This cry from love doth leap,

[29] The lover's sorrow pierces to the dividing asunder of soul and body. The unity of life is gone, and the "spirits," *i.e.*, the faculties of sense, go mourning always, because the "soul," the higher life, as distinct from the "heart," which represents the lower, their guide and companion, is no longer with them. The misery is one which God only knows, which He alone pities.

[43] The image of Beatrice is still present to his soul, more beautiful

Who vexeth me as he is wont to do,
Though less pain doth ensue,
Because the nerves of sense less keenness show, 55
And I am nearer now to end my woe.

The day, when she in this my world appeared,—
As stands in record true,
In tablets of the mind that now doth fail,—
My childish frame a strange emotion shared, 60
A passion keen and new,
So that it left me full of fear and frail:
For all my strength a curb did countervail,
So suddenly that on the earth I fell,
By reason of a voice that smote my heart: 65
And if the book truth tell,
The ruling spirit felt such trembling breath,
That it would seem that Death
Had, for it, ta'en in this our world new start:
Now is he sorely grieved who caused this smart. 70

When the great beauty first upon me shone,
Which wrought so great a pain,—
Ye gentle ladies, unto whom I spoke,—
That virtue which hath highest praises won,
Its joy beholding plain, 75

than ever, and therefore inflicting fresh pangs of self-reproach, of which the only mitigation is that her lover's strength is failing, and that therefore the overstrained nerves are less sensitive than they were; that he is also, it may be, nearing the bourne which is the end of all such sorrow.

57 Memory goes back to the hour when Beatrice first rose upon the world of the poet's life, and reproduces what we read in the opening chapter of the *V. N.* (comp. *Par.* xxiii. 14). The "ruling spirit" is, as in *V. N.* c. 2, the reasoning faculty of the soul. Here one interpreter has seen something like a parable of the history of the human race in its strivings after wisdom. "He" in l. 70 = Love.

74 The "virtue" which "wins highest praises" is, as before, the

Felt that new trouble thence upon it broke;
And knew the keen desire that in it woke,
Through what it wrought of fixèd gaze and
strong;
So that with tears it said unto the rest:
"Here will arrive ere long 80
Beauty, in place of that which I had seen,
Which worketh terror keen;
And she as queen shall be by us confest,
Soon as her eyes with joy our souls have
blest."

To you have I thus spoken, ladies young, 85
Who have bright eyes all beautiful and fair,
And mind by love subdued and sorrowful;
Wherefore extend your care
To these my words wherever they may be;
And in your presence grant I pardon free, 90
For this my death, to her so beautiful,
Who, though she caused it, ne'er was pitiful.

intellect which felt, even at the outset, that that moment of supremest joy was also the beginning of a lifelong sorrow. Life had lost its freedom, and was subject henceforth to the tyranny of a master-passion. I take l. 81 to refer to the form of the grown-up Beatrice, as taking the place of the child whose beauty had at first won him, and not to the Casentino lady, nor the *donna gentile*.

91 Is this only the poetic licence of an appeal *ad misericordiam*, or may we infer from it, as from *Canz.* i., that the over-wrought brain of the lover saw in his actual weakness the prognostic of an early death? I incline to the latter view. Comp. *n.* on l. 43.

SONNET X

THE BIRTH OF LOVE

Amor e cor gentil sono una cosa

Love and the gentle heart are one in kind,
As the wise Master in his verses wrote:
Nor one without the other may we find,
As without reason reasoning soul is not.
When Nature waxeth loving in her mind, 5
Love she makes Lord, the heart his chosen spot,
Within awhile deep slumber doth him blind,
For little time or long, as fates allot:
Then in some wise fair dame doth beauty come,
Which so doth please the eye, that in the heart 10
Springs up desire for that so great delight;

SONNET X

2 From *V. N.* c. 20. Dante had been asked by a friend to tell him something of the nature and genesis of love, and this is his answer. The sage is Guido Guinicelli (so Juvenal is a "sage," *Conv.* iv. 13), one of whose sonnets begins with the words—

"*Al cor gentil ripara sempre amore,*
Siccome augello in selva alla verdura."

"Still to the gentle heart doth Love repair
As bird doth to the greenwood's leafy screen;
Not before gentle heart has Love e'er been,
Nor gentle heart before that Love was there;"

and whom Dante recognised as the most honoured of his masters ("*Maximus Guido,*" *V. E.* i. 15) in Italian poetry (*Purg.* xi. 97, xxvi. 977; and *Essay on Genesis and Growth of the Commedia*). An echo of C. i. meets us in *H.* v. 100.

9 What Dante includes in gentleness of heart is as the good soil in

And sometimes so long while finds there a
home,
It bids Love's spirit wake to bear its part:
And so on lady fair works valiant knight.

SONNET XI

BEATRICE'S SALUTATION

Negli occhi porta la mia donna Amore

My Lady beareth Love in her fair eyes,
And by it all she sees doth noble make;
As she doth pass, all turn for her dear sake;
The man she greeteth thrills in ecstacies,
And bending low, grows pale as one that dies, 5
And mourns for every least defect he hath,
And from her presence flee false pride and
wrath;
Help me, fair ladies, to her praise to rise;

which love sows the promise and potency of life. Visible beauty, as in Plato's *Phædrus*, wakens a desire which may be spiritual or sensual, and turns the promise into a reality. What comes to pass in the heart of man has its counterpart in the heart of woman.

SONNET XI

From *V. N.* c. 21. Growing out of *S.* x. and embodying the recollections of *V. N.* c. 2, as *Canz.* ii. 57 does those of *V. N.* c. 3. The poet gives, as it were, an experimental instance of the truth which he had just uttered. So it had been with him. So it might be with others. Beatrice's salutation made all good thoughts stir within her adorer's mind, and was the beginning of his blessedness, so that then he knew why she was named Beatrice ("*nomen et omen*"); but when she smiled, the rapture was beyond speech or

All sweetness, and all lowliness of thought
Springs up within the heart that hears her speech, 10
And the first sight of her brings sense of bliss;
But when she doth a little smile, O this
May not be told, nor memory this can teach,
So new and fair a miracle is wrought.

SONNET XII

BEATRICE'S SORROW (1)

Voi, che portate la sembianza umile

O YE, who, with a mien of lowliness,
And with bent glances testify your woe,
Whence come ye that your pallid look doth show,
As though it pitying looked upon distress?

memory. So in *Par.* xviii. 8–12, xxix. 7, her smiles are reserved till the purified spirit is able to endure them (comp. *Canz.* ii. 5). Here, however, a new element comes in, and Dante dwells on the power of beauty to awaken the potency of love, even in a heart that had not before been "gentle." It can prepare the soil as well as sow the seed.

SONNET XII

From *V. N.* c. 22. Beatrice's father, Folco dei Portinari, had died (Dec. 1289), and she was overwhelmed with sorrow. Her friends came to her to comfort her, and Dante met them as they left the house (apparently he stood outside, not far off, that he might intercept them), and asked for tidings of her in words which are embodied in the Sonnet. If we ask, as it is natural to ask, where her husband was at this time of sorrow, the probable answer is, "in Paris, or in London, or Somerset, attending to his banking business" (comp. *Par.* xv. 120, *n.*).

Saw ye our Lady in her gentleness, 5
Her face all bathed in tears of love that flow?
Tell me, O ladies;—my heart tells me so—
For no base act doth look of yours express.
And if ye come from scene so piteous,
I pray you that with me awhile you stay, 10
Nor hide from me what chance doth grieve you thus:
For I behold your eyes that weep alway,
And see your looks so changed and tremulous,
That seeing this my heart too faints away.

SONNET XIII

BEATRICE'S SORROW (2)

Se' tu colui c' ha trattato sovente

"And art thou he, who hath so often sung
Of our dear Lady, telling us alone?
Like him indeed thou art in voice and tone,
But thy face seems to strange expression strung.
And why so deeply is thy bosom wrung, 5
That thou mak'st others pity feel for thee?
Hast thou seen her weep, that thou art not free
To hide thy soul's grief with a silent tongue?

SONNET XIII

From *V. N.* c. 22. The friends of Beatrice make answer to the lover's question, and tell him of her depth of grief. They note that he himself is so transformed by sorrow that they could scarcely recognise him.

Leave tears to us, and mournful movement
slow,—
He sins who seeks our trouble to console,— 10
For, as she wept, we heard her speech too flow:
So plain her looks betray her sorrowing soul,
That whoso would have sought to gauge her woe
Had fallen down and bowed to death's
control."

SONNET XIV

THE COMPANY OF MOURNERS

Voi, donne, che pietoso atto mostrate

"Ye ladies, who the mien of pity show,
Who is this lady that lies grief-opprest?
Can it be she who in my heart doth rest?
Ah! if it be, no longer hide it so.
Truly her features are so changed by woe, 5
And her face seems to me so worn and spent,
That in mine eyes she doth not represent
Her from whom power to bless was wont to
flow."

SONNET XIV

Not in the *V. N.*, but apparently connected with the same episode as *S.* xii. and xiii., embodying another question and another answer. Had Dante seen his beloved one prostrate on the ground, her eyes red with weeping, her face pale with watching? The brightness and the smiles were gone. Was she the same? "Yes," the wise ladies answer. "Yea," he makes answer to himself, "she is identified by her gentleness and calmness."

"If thou canst not our Lady recognise,
So downcast is she, 'tis no wonder great, 10
Since the same thing has happened to our eyes;
But if thou look well, by the light sedate
Of her calm glance fresh knowledge shall arise:
Weep then no more: too sad, e'en now, thy state."

SONNET XV

WHAT TIDINGS OF BEATRICE?

Onde venite voi così pensose

Whence come ye thus with trouble so o'er-wrought?
Tell me, I pray you, of your courtesy;
For I am full of doubt, lest it may be
My Lady makes you turn thus sorrow-fraught.
Al., gentle ladies, let no scornful thought 5
Keep you from pausing somewhat on your way,
And to the mourner fail ye not to say
If ye of his fair Lady-love know aught,
Though it be grievous for me that to hear.
So far as Love from himself banished me, 10
That every act of his brings death more near.
Look well, and whether I am wasted see,
For every sense begins to leave its sphere,
If ye, O ladies, give not comfort free.

SONNET XV

Yet another utterance of the same time of sorrow. Cannot the

CANZONE IV

FOREBODINGS

Donna pietosa e di novella etate

A LADY pitiful, in youth's fresh bloom,
And furnished well with human gentleness
Was nigh, when often I on Death did call,
And she mine eyes beholding full of gloom,
And hearing those my words of vain distress, 5
Was moved to fear, and tears began to fall;
And other ladies, who did me perceive,
Through her who mingled thus her grief with mine,
Bade her elsewhere incline,
And then approached me so that I might hear. 10
This said, "Sleep thou not here."
Another, "Wherefore doth thy soul thus grieve?"
Then rose I from that new-born fantasy,
And on my Lady's name was fain to cry.

gentle ladies with whom he has conversed give him some tidings of his Beatrice? Even if those tidings should be sorrowful, it will be better than the blank uncertainty of hearing nothing. For "courtesy" (l. 2) see *H.* ii. 58, *n.*

CANZONE IV.

From *V. N.* c. 23. We enter on a strain of higher mood. The tension implied in the last four Sonnets had ended in actual illness. The lover took to his bed, suffering severe pain for nine days; his mind wandered; there was the risk of a brain-fever. A cousin, or perhaps sister, young, fair, gentle, came and sat by his side, weeping as he called on death to end his sorrows. Other ladies followed, and bade her leave him. What came next the Canzone records, the mind at last finding power and leisure to make a psychological study of its own delirium. He notes (l. 14) that he would not audibly utter Beatrice's name.

13 In the first anguish of that delirium Dante had called on death

So sorrowful and sad my voice became, 15
And broken so with anguish and with woe,
That I alone the name heard in my heart;
And with my face suffused with blush of shame
Which over all my features 'gan to flow,
Love made me turn to them, nor stand apart. 20
Such pallid hue my countenance then bore,
It made them speak of me as one half-dead,
"Come, let us comfort shed."
One prayed another in deep lowliness;
And thus would questions press: 25
"What hast thou seen that thou art strong no more?"
And when some comfort o'er my soul was spread,
"Dear ladies, I will tell you all," I said.

"While with sad thoughts my frail life I did weigh,
And dwelt upon its days so short and few, 30
Love wept within my heart which is his home:
Wherefore my spirit went so far astray,
That sighing through my heart the whisper flew,
'E'en to my Lady death will surely come.'
Then did my soul in such strange wanderings roam, 35

(l. 3). The questions of his visitors rouse him, and he calls on Beatrice, but the cry is still inaudible. They gaze alarmed at his sudden flush and equally sudden pallor. "What has caused it?"

34 Many readers will remember Wordsworth's unconscious parallelism—

"'Ah mercy!' to myself I cried,
'If Lucy should be dead!'"

Not many months had passed before the prophecy was fulfilled.

I closed mine eyes beneath their sorrow's
weight;
And so disconsolate
Were all my senses that each failed and fled.
And then by fancy led
Beyond all knowledge, where Truth's voice is
dumb, 40
Fair ladies' faces sorrowing met mine eye,
Who said to me: 'Thou too shalt die, shalt
die.'

"Then saw I many things that made me muse.
In that vain dream wherein I then was led.
I deemed I found myself I know not where, 45
And saw fair dames pass by with tresses loose.
One sobbed for grief; another salt tears shed,
All darted fire of sorrow and despair.
Then step by step it seemed that I saw there
The sun grow dark, and stars begin to peep, 50
And that with these did weep:
The birds fell down as they their flight did
take;
The earth began to quake;
And one came saying, hoarse and full of care:
'What, know'st thou not our news of sorrow
deep? 55
Thy Lady, once so fair, in death doth sleep.'

Was this, too, among Dante's morning dreams? (*H.* xxvi. 7; *Purg.* ix. 16.) With that foreboding of his lady's death there came a like anticipation of his own.

42 As in *S.* viii., the echoes of the cries of the Sicilian Vespers are still ringing in his ears (*Par.* viii. 75), and they seem spoken to him.

45 The vision of Beatrice's funeral comes before him, and the whole world is darkened.

"Then lifting up mine eyes all bathed in woe,
Angels I saw, who seemed a rain of manna,
And turning, upwards winged to Heaven their flight;
And a small cloud in front of them did go; 60
And all behind it went and cried 'Hosanna.'
Had they said more I would have told you right;
Then Love said, 'I'll not hide it from thy sight;
Come see thy Lady as she there doth lie.'
Then dream-like phantasy 65
Led me upon my lady dead to look,
And as a glance I took,
Fair dames were wrapping her in cere-cloth white;
And with her was such true humility,
It seemed as though she said, 'In peace am I.' 70

"And I became so humble in my woe,
Seeing in her such full lowliness exprest,
I said 'O Death, I find thee passing sweet:
Needs must thou as a thing all gentle show,
Since with my Lady thou hast been a guest, 75
And pity in thee, not disdain, were meet.
Behold, that I with such strong wish entreat

68 The transfiguration, one might almost say the apotheosis, of Beatrice coincides not with her actual death, but with the first vision of it. We have an anticipation of her glory as she appears in *Purg.* xxxi. 143. The "desire of the saints and angels" (*Canz.* ii. 15–21) is satisfied, and the calm beauty of her corpse bears witness that she is at peace. He had longed for death, if death were like that. Wailing was over, and then his friends had come, and "behold, it was a dream!" Did the poet reproduce the symbolism of mediæval art, in which the departing soul appeared as a child borne up to Heaven in a bright cloud? Line 80, as interpreted by the prose narrative, may be rendered, "When all due rites were done."

To be of thine that I like thee may be;
  Come, for my heart calls thee.'
Then I departed, all my wailing done; 80
  And when I was alone,
I said, with glance upraised to Heaven's high
    seat:
'Blessed is he, fair Soul, who thee doth see!'
And then ye called me of your charity."

SONNET XVI

GIOVANNA AND BEATRICE

Io mi sentii svegliar dentro allo core

I FELT within, awakening in my heart,
  A loving spirit that had slept till then,
  And then I saw Love from afar off start
(So blithe that scarce I knew his face again),

SONNET XVI.

From *V. N.* c. 24. As in *S.* ii., Vanna, the beloved of Guido Cavalcanti, and Beatrice appear in close companionship. The former was known, it tells us, as the *Primavera,* or Spring, on account of her beauty. The latter, as in *Sonn.* iii. 10, he identifies with Love itself. The shortened form "*Bice*" appears in *Sonn.* ii. 9, in *Par.* vii. 14, and in the will of her father, Folco dei Portinari. The poet's fancy plays on Giovanna, (1) as meaning in Hebrew (Jochanan) the grace of God; (2) as being derived from the name of the forerunner of One greater than himself, even as Vanna went before Beatrice; (3) as having in the name commonly given her (*Primavera*=*prima verra*=she will come first) the witness of that relation. The whole conception, measured by our standard, seems singularly fantastic; but those who have entered into the fulness of Dante's ripened powers will recognise, if I mistake not, that this efflorescence of ingenuity in tracking remote analogies and the

And said: "In honouring me do now thy part," 5
And at each word he still to smile was fain.
And as my Lord and I some time apart
Stood, looking thither whence he came, full
plain,
I Lady Vanna, Lady Bicè, saw
Come nigh towards the spot where I stood
there, 10
One close upon the other miracle;
And e'en as now my thoughts true record draw,
Love said to me, "This is the Springtide fair,
And Love, the other's name, let likeness tell."

SONNET XVII

"BEATRICE, GOD'S TRUE PRAISE"

Tanto gentile e tanto onesta pare

So gentle and so fair she seems to be,
My Lady, when she others doth salute,
That every tongue becomes, all trembling,
mute,
And every eye is half afraid to see;

mystic significance of names was an element eminently characteristic. The meaning of Giovanna, *e.g.*, is specially dwelt on in *Par.* xii. 80. The Sonnet was addressed, he says, to his "chief friend," *i.e.*, to Guido Cavalcanti.

SONNET XVII

From *V. N.* c. 26. Hitherto the lover had spoken chiefly of the impression made by Beatrice on himself. Now his words take a

She goes her way and hears men's praises free, [5]
Clothed in a garb of kindness, meek and low,
And seems as if from heaven she came, to show
Upon the earth a wondrous mystery.
To one who looks on her she seems so kind,
That through the eyes a sweetness fills the heart, [10]
Which only he can know who doth it try.
And through her face there breatheth from her mind
A spirit sweet and full of Love's true art,
Which to the soul saith, as it cometh, "Sigh."

wider range. He will tell of the impression made on others. Whatever allowance we make for the hyperboles of love, the Sonnet may be received as evidence that Dante was not alone in his admiration, that Beatrice left on all her friends—and her father's and her husband's position probably brought all the notables of Florence, its men of culture and wealth and rank, within her circle —the impression of an angel-like perfection. In her presence the strife of tongues ceased, and the mockers were hushed into a reverential silence by that stainless purity. Spenser's Una, in the region of imagination, the devout and "gracious" Lady Margaret Maynard, who was Ken's Beatrice (*n.* on *Purg.* xxxi. 22) in that of reality, supply suggestive parallels. Some of us may have known, in the quiet life of Hurstmonceaux Rectory, one who left a like impression on those who came in contact with her—not to enter on the inner circle of her home-life—from Arthur Stanley, Archbishop Trench, and Cardinal Manning, to John Sterling, Walter Savage Landor, and George Eliot. "Face" for "*labbia*" is justified (l. 12) by *H.* vii. 7; *Purg.* xxiii. 47.

SONNET XVIII

THE BEAUTY OF HOLINESS

Vede perfettamente ogni salute

He sees completely fullest bliss abound
  Who among ladies sees my Lady's face;
  Those that with her do go are surely bound
To give God thanks for such exceeding grace.
And in her beauty such strange might is found, 5
  That envy finds in other hearts no place;
  So she makes them walk with her, clothed all
      round
With love and faith and courteous gentleness.
The sight of her makes all things lowly be;
  Nor of herself alone she gives delight, 10
  But each through her receiveth honour due.
And in her acts is such great courtesy,
  That none can recollect that wondrous sight,
  Who sighs not for it in Love's sweetness true.

SONNET XVIII.

The influence of the angelic presence is pursued still further. Her companions are, as it were, radiant with her reflected light, and are better for her presence. The woman whom many men admire, who makes many "conquests," is seldom a favourite with her own sex. With Beatrice it was otherwise, and men and women alike loved and reverenced her.

SONNET XIX

ALL SAINTS' DAY, 1289

Di donne io vidi una gentile schiera

I SAW a band of gentle dames pass by,
  Upon the morn of this last All Saints' Day,
  And one came on, as chief in dignity,
And on her right hand Love himself did stay.
A ray of light she darted from her eye, 5
  Which, like a burning spirit, made its way:
  And I, such boldness had I, could descry
Her features fair an angel's face display.
To him who worthy was she greeting gave
  With her bright eyes, that Lady good and
    kind, 10
Filling the heart of each with valour brave.
  In heaven I deem that she her birth did find,
And came upon the earth us men to save,
  And blest is she who follows close behind.

SONNET XIX

Not in the *V. N.* It was probably the last All-Saints' Day (Nov. 1, 1289) of Beatrice's life. We see her as she went with a company of friends to the *festa*, probably in the Church of Ognissanti, Dante watching them, seeking to catch the "*salute*" which was his *salute* (in the Italian the word in its twofold sense rhymes with itself), and made him braver and truer than it found him. The day was one much to be remembered, all the more so when Beatrice herself was numbered with the saints.

12 Comp. *S.* xvii. 7.

BALLATA V

DAWNING OF NEW HOPE

Deh Nuvoletta, che in ombra d' Amore

AH Cloud, that, in Love's shadow sweeping past,
  Hast suddenly appeared before mine eyes,
  Have pity on the heart which wounded lies,
Which hopes in thee, yet, yearning, dies at last.
Thou Cloud, in beauty more than human
    seen, 5
  A fire hast kindled in my inmost heart,
    With speech of thine that slays;

Then, with a glowing spirit's act and art,
  Thou genderest hope, which doth to healing
    lean,
    When I on thy smile gaze, 10
  Ah, seek not why a new trust it doth raise,
  But on my yearning look, whose fire is strong;
  Ere now a thousand dames, through tarrying
    long,
Have felt on them the grief of others cast.

BALLATA V

In the vision of *Canz.* iv. 60, the soul of Beatrice had been seen rising to heaven as in a cloud (comp. *H.* xxvi. 37; *Purg.* xxx. 28), and that thought is the starting-point of the present poem. Here, as in *Sonn.* iii. and xvi., she is identified with Love himself. That vision of glory haunts him. The words that fall from it pierce his soul, yet they bring hope, and therefore, like the spear of the Greek hero, heal as well as smite.

SONNET XX

CREDENTIALS WITHDRAWN

O dolci rime, che parlando andate

DEAR rhymes, who, as ye go, hold converse sweet
Of that fair dame who wins for others praise:
To you will come, perhaps with you now stays,
One ye will doubtless as your brother greet.
I, that ye list not to him, you entreat, 5
By that Lord who in ladies love doth raise;
For in his utterance dwelleth there always
A thing that is for Truth no comrade meet.
And if ye should be moved by words of his
To seek her presence whom as yours ye own, 10
Stay not your steps, but to her feet draw
nigher,
And say, "O Lady, we have thus come on
To speak for one who all his joy doth miss,
Saying, 'Where is she whom my fond eyes
desire?'"

SONNET XX

Not in the *V. N.* The drift is so far clear that we see at once that the Sonnet is of the nature of a recantation. The poems which represent the lover's true self are not to admit one which will come as claiming to be of their company. He is not a faithful messenger, does not speak the poet's true mind. I surmise that *Sonn.* vii., with its tone of somewhat petulant complaint, may have been that which Dante sought to disclaim.

SONNET XXI

REPULSION AND ATTRACTION

Dagli occhi della mia donna si muove

From my dear Lady's eyes a light doth gleam,
So clear and noble that, where it doth shine,
Things are revealed no artist can define,
Lofty and strange beyond all fancy's dream.
And from their rays upon my heart doth
stream 5
Such fear, it thrills through all my nerves
and brain,
And I say, "Here I will not turn again."
But soon my fixed resolves abandoned seem;
And there I turn whence cometh my dismay,
To find some comfort for my timorous eyes, 10
Which erst that might and majesty did own:
When I arrive, ah me! their vision dies,
And the desire which led them fades away;
Wherefore let Love's care for my state be
shown.

SONNET XXI

No interest of circumstance, not much perhaps of any kind, attaches to what is but one of the variations on the lover's ever-recurring theme. *S.* viii. and *S.* xi. may be compared with it, as illustrating the subtle skill and delicacy of such variations. Its vagueness and that of *S.* xxii. may perhaps be connected with the fact that they were written ostensibly for the "screen" lady of *V. N.* c. 5.

SONNET XXII

THE MOTH AND THE CANDLE

Io son si vago della bella luce

I AM so eager for the beauteous light
Of those fair traitor eyes that me have slain,
That thither, whence I have my scorn and pain,
I am led back by that my great delight:
And that which clear, or less clear, meets my sight 5
So dazzles both my soul's and body's eye
That, both from thought and virtue parted, I
Follow desire alone as leader right.
And he doth lead me on, so full of trust,
To pleasant death by pleasant fraud brought on, 10
I only know it when the harm is done.
And much I grieve for grief that scorn hath won,
But most I murmur, ah! for so I must,
That pity too is robbed of guerdon just.

SONNET XXII

The authorship has been assigned to Dante's friend Cino da Pistoia, but it is received as Dante's own by *Frat.*, *Witt.*, and others. Internal evidence is, I think, in its favour.

CANZONE V

"THE FEAR OF DEATH IS FALLEN UPON ME"

Morte, poich' io non truovo a cui mi doglia

DEATH, since I find not one who with me grieves,
None in whom pity for me moveth sighs,
Where turn mine eyes, or wheresoe'er I
stay;
And since that thou art he who me bereaves
Of all my strength, and robes in miseries, 5
Till on me rise misfortune's blackest day;
Since thou, O Death, canst, as thy will may
sway,
Make my life rich, or plunge in poverty,
'Tis meet that I should turn my face to thee,
Portrayed like face where Death paints every
line; 10
To thee, as piteous friend, I make my way,
Wailing, O Death, that sweet tranquillity
Thy stroke takes from me, if it robbeth me
Of that fair dame who with her heart bears
mine,
Who of all good is portal true and shrine 15

CANZONE V.

Not in the *V. N.* We are left in no room for doubt as to the date and occasion of this *Canzone*. It was obviously written in the early days of June 1290, when Beatrice was hovering between life and death. The prophetic vision of *Canz.* iv. was nearing its fulfilment, and the poet turns to Death with an appeal for pity, asking, if it may be, for some short respite ere the angels gain their wish (*Canz.* ii. 15–23). Line 56 shows that the apotheosis of Beatrice is still the dominant thought in her lover's mind. It is suggestive that the Canzone is found in a Breslau MS. prefixed to the *Commedia* by way of introduction.

Death, what may be the peace thou tak'st from
me,
Bewailing which to thee in tears I come,
Of this I'm dumb; for thou canst see it
well,
If thou mine eyes all wet with weeping see,
Or see the grief that in them finds its home, 20
Or see the doom, of death so visible.
Ah, if fear now with strokes so keen and fell
Hath thus dealt with me, what will anguish
do,
If I see Death her eyes' clear light subdue,
That wont to be to mine so sweet a guide! 25
That thou dost seek mine end I clearly tell,
Great joy to thee from my woe will accrue:
For much I fear, as feeling that dread spell,
Lest, that I might by lesser grief be tried,
I should seek death, and none would death
provide. 30

Death, if thou smite this gentle lady fair,
Whose supreme virtue to the intellect
Shows as perfect what in her we may view,
Virtue thou driv'st to exile and despair,
Thou tak'st from grace the home that doth
protect, 35
And high effect dost rob of honour due;
Thou wreckest all her beauteous form and hue,
Which shines with more of good than others
shine,
As that must needs do which brings light
divine
From heaven in form of creature worthiest.
Thou break'st and crushest all the good
faith true 40

Of that truth-loving Love who guides her right;
If thou, O Death, dost quench her lovely
light,
Love may well say where'er his sway doth
rest,
"Lo! I have lost my banner, fairest, best."

Death, grieve thou now for that exceeding ill, 45
So sure to follow if my loved One dies;
Which all men's eyes as greatest woe will
own.
Slacken thy bow that in it linger still
The arrow that upon the string yet lies,
Which thou dost poise, its aim her heart
alone; 50
For pity's sake, look to it ere 'tis done.
Curb thou a little while thine uncurbed rage,
Now stirred against her life thy war to wage,
To whom God giveth such exceeding grace.
Ah! Death, if thou hast pity, be it shown 55
Without delay. I see Heaven's heritage
Open; God's angels to our lower stage
Descend, to bear that blest soul to the place
Where hymn and song do honour to her
grace.

Canzon', thou see'st how subtle is the thread, 60
On which doth hang my hopes that slender
be,
How strength doth flee without my Lady fair.
Wherefore, I pray thee, softly, gently tread,
My little song, nor slack to ope thy plea,
For upon thee dependeth all my prayer, 65
And, with that lowly mien thou'rt wont to
bear,

Seek thou Death's presence now, my little
song,
That thou may'st shatter fierce wrath's
portals strong,
And gain the meed of worthy fruits of love:
And if by thee he may be moved to spare 70
That doom of death, take heed thou stay
not long
To bear thy comfort for my Lady's wrong,
So that to this our world she bounteous
prove,
That gentle Soul, for whom I live and move.

STANZA

SIGHS FOR BEATRICE'S GREETING

Si lungamente m' ha tenuto Amore

So long have I been prisoner held by Love,
And thus trained to endure his sovereignty,
That as, before, he harsh was found to me,
So now he stays, my heart's sweet guest to
prove.

STANZA

From the *V. N.* c. 28. Not a Sonnet, though it commonly appears with that title, but rather, as Dante himself tells, the first verse of a *Canzone* which was interrupted by the death of Beatrice, and the burden of which was the lover's desire for the greeting which, for some cause, possibly the illness which ended fatally, he had missed. For us the fragment has the interest of giving the last lines written to the living Beatrice.

Wherefore, when he my courage doth re-
move, 5
So that my spirits seem far off to flee,
Such sense of sweetness then comes over me,
That my frail soul with pallid face doth rove.
O'er me then Love such mastery doth show,
He sets my sighs afloat, with speech endowed; 10
And they cry out aloud
On my dear Lady, greeting to bestow.
This happens whensoe'er she looks on me,
So lowly, passing all belief, is she.

CANZONE VI

BEATRICE IN PARADISE

Gli occhi dolenti per pietà del core

My sorrowing eyes, through pity for my mind,
Have through their weeping suffered pain so
great,
That now they stop, their tears all spent and
gone;
Whence, if an opening I for grief would find
That leads me, step by step, to Death's
estate, 5

CANZONE VI

1-2 (From *V. N.* c. 32.) The blow has at last fallen, and we can understand from *Canz.* v. what its first effect must have been. Critics who cannot "fathom" the "poet's mind," and therefore "vex" it with their "shallow wit," have made merry over the letter beginning with the words of *Lam.* i. 1, which the young lover

Needs must I speak with many a sigh and groan.
And since I call to mind that I was known
Of my dear Lady, while she lived, to tell,
Ye gentle ladies, willingly with you,
I seek not hearers new, 10
But to the kind hearts that in ladies dwell
Will I now speak, while tears my cheeks bedew,
Since she hath gone to Heaven thus suddenly,
And leaves Love mourning in my company.

Into high Heaven hath Beatricè passed, 15
That kingdom where the angels find their peace,
And dwells with them; from you, fair dames, doth fly.
It was not spell of cold that killed at last,
Nor that of heat, that other lives bids cease,

addressed to "all the princes of the land." Give these words their true meaning, "to all the chief men of Florence," and I cannot see anything in the act so supremely ridiculous. Tennyson's *In Memoriam* has taught us how a perfectly sane poet may take the whole world into the sanctuary of a buried friendship. Was it strange that Dante should address an *In Memoriam* letter, afterwards expanded into such a *Canzone* as this, to the many who had shared his reverence and admiration for Beatrice, even as he had addressed the Sonnet which had told of the new beginning of his New Life to his brother poets? Of the circumstances of her death (June 9, 1290), we know but little, but that little is suggestive. It was no common consumption or fever (ll. 18, 19). Had she faded away under the pressure of a loveless and joyless marriage with a man older than herself, who left her alone in Florence while he was occupied with the foreign business of his firm in France or England? (*Par.* xv. 121 *n.*) Something she had said on her death-bed which Dante could not repeat without egotism (*V. N.* c. 29). Had she left a dying message that she, at least, had understood him, appreciated him, loved him, as far as the wife of another might love? Had she bidden him cherish the memory of that love as the safeguard of his faith and purity? This is, at least, the natural inference, and *Purg.* xxx. 103–145 goes far to confirm it. We, at all events, may note at every step prophetic anticipations of all that is most glorious in the *Commedia*.

1-14 The lover turns for sympathy to those who are mourners like himself, to whom he has before spoken of his passion (*Canz.* ii.).

16 Comp. *Par.*

18 The lines, as noted above, are sufficiently suggestive.

But her own great and sweet benignity; 20
For the clear light of her humility
Passed into heaven with such exceeding
power
It roused great wonder in the Eternal Sire,
So that a sweet desire
Came on Him to call hence so bright a
flower, 25
And bade her pass from earth and mount up
higher,
Because He saw this troublous life of care
Was all unworthy of a thing so fair.

Now hath the gentle spirit ta'en its flight
From her fair form, so full of sweetest
grace, 30
And she shines glorious in a worthy home.
Who speaks of her, and doth not weep out-
right,
Hath heart of stone so evil and so base,
That into it no spirit kind can come.
No villain heart by skill of thought can
sum 35
The measure of her excellence complete,
And thence it is he hath no will to weep;
But he great woe doth keep,
And grief and sighs that fain for death
entreat,
And from his soul all consolation sweep, 40
Who in his thoughts doth sometimes con-
template
What she was like, and what hath been her
fate.

23 An echo of *Canz.* ii. 15-21.

My many sighs work in me anguish sore,
  When in my saddened mind my troubled
      thought
  Brings back her form, whose beauty pierced
      my heart; 45
  And oftentimes, her death revolving o'er,
  There comes a longing with such sweetness
      fraught,
  It makes all colour from my face depart;
  And such pain comes to me from every part
  When this imagination holds me fast, 50
  I shudder as I feel my misery;
    And so transformed am I,
  That shame my lot apart from men has cast.
  Then weeping in my sore lament I cry
  On Beatricè, saying, "Art thou dead?" 55
  And as I call, by her I'm comforted.

Tears of great grief and sighs of anguish keen
  Sore vex my heart, when I am found alone,
  That whosoe'er beheld it, 'twould distress:
  And what the tenor of my life hath been, 60
  Since my dear Lady that new world hath won,
  There is no tongue that could in full express.
  And therefore, ladies, not through will's full
      stress
  Could I to you what now I am declare;
  Such travail sore my hard life works for me, 65
    So bowed in misery,
  Each seems to say, "I of thy life despair,"
  Seeing my cold lips death-pale with agony.
  But what I am my Lady sees full plain,
  And I still hope her pity to obtain. 70

56 Comp. the "in dreams and other ways" of *Purg.* xxx. 134.
69 Looking on Beatrice as a saint, it was but natural that he should turn to her, trusting in her pity and intercession.

Go on thy way, sad Canzon', weeping go,
  And find the ladies and the maidens fair,
  To whom thy sister songs were wont to bear
    Much joy in days gone by;
  And thou, the daughter of great misery, 75
  Take thou thy place with them in thy despair.

SONNET XXIII

GRIEF TOO DEEP FOR TEARS

Venite a intender gli sospiri miei

Come now, and listen ye to each sad sigh,
  O gentle hearts, for pity this doth pray;
  Sighs that in deepest sorrow wend their way,
And if they did not, I of grief should die.
For now mine eyes are debtors still to cry 5
  More often far than with my will doth stay,
  Weeping, ah me! my Lady passed away,
For weeping would assuage my misery.
Ye will hear them call often on the name
  Of that my gentle Lady, who hath gone 10
  Into a world for her great virtue meet,
And ofttimes scorn the life I now drag on,
  In likeness of a sorrowing spirit's frame,
  Deprived for ever of her greeting sweet.

SONNET XXIII

From *V. N.* c. 33. The history which is thus embodied is briefly told. Beatrice's brother, his dearest friend next to Guido Cavalcanti, came to him and asked him to write some verses on the death of a

CANZONE VII

BEATRICE WITH THE ANGELS

Quantunque volte (ahi lasso!) mi rimembra

AH me! as often as I call to mind
That I shall never more
See the fair Lady whom I wail and weep,
So great an inward grief my heart doth find
All gathered, heap on heap, 5
That I say, "Soul, why dost thou not depart?
For the keen torments that will vex thy heart
In that world which to thee much woe hath brought,
Fill me with saddest thoughts and anxious fear;"
So I bid Death come near, 10
As with a sweet and gentle quiet fraught,
And say "O come to me," so lovingly,
That I am envious of whoe'er doth die.

fair lady, not saying who she was. Dante, however, felt sure that it was for her he had lost, and wrote accordingly. As one point specially noticeable is the growing weariness of life in l. 12. One notes, as an instance of the possibilities of interpretation, the astounding conjecture (*Flotho*) that the friend who came to Dante was Beatrice's husband.

CANZONE VII

From *V. N.* c. 34. Written as a sequel to *S.* xxiii. That seemed to him, as he read it, inadequate for the occasion. With a curious self-analysis, he distinguishes between the first stanza as expressing the feelings of the brother, and the second as uttering his own. As one reads the *Canzone* it seems difficult to follow the distinction. He himself lays stress on the fact that the words "my Lady fair" occur only in the latter of the two stanzas. There also we may perhaps note the prominence of the apotheosis element which was so intensely personal. (Comp. *Purg.* xxx. 28–75.)

And in my sighs there comes and claims its part
  An utterance of great woe, 15
That alway calls on Death in its despair.
To him are turned all longings of my heart,
  Since she, my Lady fair,
Felt of his cruel dart the deadly blow:
Because the joys that from her beauty flow, 20
Departing far away from mortal sight,
Have grown to spirit's beauty perfected,
  Which through the heavens doth shed,
Greeting the angels, Love and Love's clear light,
And bids their subtle high intelligence 25
With wonder gaze; so great her excellence.

SONNET XXIV[1]

A YEAR AFTER

Era venuta nella mente mia

THAT gentle Lady came upon my thought
  For whom Love weeps of many tears a shower,
  Just at the point when his exceeding power
Drew you to look at that which then I wrought.

SONNET XXIV

From *V. N.* c. 35. Twelve months had passed since the great sorrow, and the *Conv.* ii. 2, 13, tells us something of Dante's inner

[1] As the Sonnet stands in the *Vita Nuova* the first four lines run thus:—

That gentle Lady on my thoughts did come
  Who for her noble and exceeding worth
  Is placed by Him, the Lord Supreme of earth,
In heaven of lowliness, our Mary's home.

Love, who to feel her presence there was
 brought, 5
 Woke up within my sad and troubled heart,
 And to my sighs said, "Up, and onward
 start."
And so they took their way, with sorrow fraught.
Weeping they issued forth from out my breast,
With such a voice as often doth collect 10
 The tears of sorrow into mourning eyes.
But those who struggled forth with most unrest,
 Went uttering still, "O noble intellect!
 A year hath passed since thou to heaven didst
 rise!"

history during them. He had turned for comfort, as a student-nature like his was likely to do, to philosophy, and in particular to Boethius, *De Consolatione Philosophiæ*, and Cicero, *De Amicitiâ*. The necessarily heathen character of the latter book and the absolutely non-Christian character of the former led him away from the truest and deepest source of consolation. He entered on what has been called the second stage of the Trilogy of his life, on the whole, one of a falling away from his first love, and perhaps also from his first purity (*Purg.* xxx. 115-145). When the anniversary of the fatal day, however, came round, as he was sketching the form of an angel (this implies that he had turned to art studies also by way of relief, probably in company with Giotto under Cimabue), his work was interrupted by visitors, and then, when they had left him, the picture of the angel he had lost rose up before him, and his sorrow found vent in sighs.

As at first written, the first four lines ran thus—

"That gentle lady in my thoughts did come
 Who, for her noble and exceeding worth,
 Is placed by Him, the Lord of heaven and earth,
In heaven of lowliness, the Virgin's home."

Line 4 is interesting as anticipating *H.* ii. 94, and *Par.* xxxii. 9.

One notes, I think, in the Sonnet as it stands, in spite of its infinite pathos, a certain falling off in loftiness of aspiration. Sorrow hardly seems to be doing its strengthening and ennobling work. Even the substituted four lines speak a more philosophical, but less devotional feeling than those of which they took the place. So in the last, he thinks of his Beatrice rather as a "supreme intellect" than as an angel or a saint.

SONNET XXV

THE RELIEF OF TEARS

Videro gli occhi miei quanta pietate

Mine eyes beheld what pity deep and true
  Was in thy look and features manifest,
  When on those acts and mien thy glance did
    rest,
Which sorrow in me often doth renew.
Then I perceived how all thy thoughts did view 5
  The state of this my life so dark and drear,
  So that there sprang within my heart a fear
Lest with mine eyes I should my weakness show ;

SONNET XXV

From *V. N.* c. 36. The poet was alone in his chamber, sad and lonely, when he looked out and saw a fair young face, pale as Beatrice had been, watching him with looks of pity. Some, *e.g.*, Sir Theodore Martin, have conjectured that it was Gemma Donati, whom he afterwards married, and have built up what one may call a Dante-Grandison romance. Pity grows into love. He tells Gemma his story, asks her to accept his hand and the "widowed heart" which can never be wholly hers, and so they are married. I cannot say that I think this even a probable conjecture. It would probably have been better for Dante's happiness had there been that foundation of sympathy in his marriage. Curiously enough, in the *Convito* he identifies the "gentle lady" with Philosophy, and hence a host of commentators, mostly those who reduce Beatrice to a shadowy symbol, have denied her any historical personality. I agree with Witte and Krafft that the theory of the *Convito* was an after-thought, with just so much foundation in fact as that, having begun to idealise Beatrice as representing Divine Wisdom, it seemed to him natural to identify the "gentle lady" with the human wisdom of his philosophical teachers. It seems to me simply impossible to read the *V. N.* and believe that either of the two was altogether a phantom of the brain, though in the crucible of his imagination they might be sublimated till they appeared so to others, and even to himself. I incline to the belief that the "gentle lady" is the "*Pargoletta*," the "girl of little price," of *Purg.* xxxi. 59, but do not assume that the affection passed beyond a so-called platonic

And I removed me from thee, feeling deep
Within me, that my heart's sad tears would flow, 10
Which in thy presence sweet their impulse found.
Then in my sad soul did a cry resound,
"Now with this lady dear that Love doth go,
Who makes me thus to wend my way and weep."

SONNET XXVI

SORROW FINDING SYMPATHY

Color d' amore e di pietà sembianti

Love's pallid hue and sorrow's signs of woe
Never laid hold with such a wondrous might
On lady fair, when looking on the sight
Of lowly eyes and mournful tears that flow,

sentimentalism, and believe that Beatrice's reproaches cover both the literal and the allegorical meaning.

SONNET XXVI

From *V. N.* c. 37. The presence of the gentle lady recalled the paleness, the looks, and movements of Beatrice. They called tears to his eyes, and yet as long as he looked on her he could not weep. So when he came to allegorise, he may have seen in Philosophy a kind of sister-likeness—*qualis decet esse sororum*—to the higher wisdom of Theology. For "the hue of love" compare "*Palleat omnis amans, pallens color aptus amanti.*" Ovid, *Ars Amandi*, i. 729; and "*Tinctus viola pallor amantium,*" Hor., *Od.* iii, 10, 14.

As then on thine when first thou cam'st to
know 5
My face, where grief its record sad did write,
So that through thee did on my mind alight
A thought which will, I fear, my heart o'er-
throw.
I cannot keep mine eyes, o'erspent with grief,
From turning often upon thee their gaze, 10
In the keen longing that they have to weep:
And thou that wish to such a height dost raise
That they are wasted, finding no relief,
And yet thy presence tears from them doth
keep.

SONNET XXVII

THE WANDERINGS OF THE EYES

L'amaro lagrimar che voi faceste

"The many bitter tears ye made me shed,
O eyes of mine, so long a season's space,
Made others look with wonder on my case,
In this my grief, as ye have witnessèd.

SONNET XXVII

From *V. N.* c. 38. We have a phase of feeling which indicates that the first love is losing its power. It was wrong to forget the past, yet the present had its attractions, and, as they drew him to one who shared the memories of the past, was it not possible to reconcile the two?

He represents himself in the prose of the *V. N.* as reproaching his eyes because they looked on the living form of the "lady of the window," instead of weeping for Beatrice, as they had done before.

But in you now oblivion soon were bred, 5
Had I on my part been so caitiff base,
Not from you all occasion to efface,
Reminding you of her ye weep as dead.
Your fickle wanderings cause me many a groan
And so alarm me, that in truth I dread 10
The face of lady fair that looks on you.
Never should ye our Lady who is dead
Forget, till death claims you too as his own."
So speaks my heart, and thereat sighs anew.

SONNET XXVIII

PITY AKIN TO LOVE

Gentil pensiero, che parla di vui

A GENTLE thought, which speaks to me of thee,
Within me cometh oftentimes to stay,
And doth of Love such sweet discourse display,
It makes my heart with it in sympathy.
My soul saith to my heart, "Who may this be, 5
That to our mind comes comfort to convey,
And hath in virtue such a potent sway
That other thoughts from us afar must flee?"

SONNET XXVIII

From *V. N.* c. 39. The new love is growing stronger, and is driving out the old. There is at least a drifting towards an entire transfer of affection. The Sonnet is, as he says in the *V. N.*, the outcome of a "battle of thought" between the soul (the higher reason) and the "heart," which yields to the passing emotions, and the consolations which the latter offers the former rejects as utterly vile and unworthy.

The heart replies, "O soul so sorrowful,
  This is a spirit, new and young, of Love, 10
  Who brings before me all his fond desires:
And all his life and all his virtue move
  From the fair eyes of her so pitiful,
  Who oft hath grieved o'er our consuming fires.

SONNET XXIX

SIGHS AND THOUGHTS

Lasso! per forza de' molti sospiri

Ah me! by reason of the many sighs,
  Which spring from thoughts that dwell within
    my heart,
  Mine eyes are spent, and lose their former art
To meet, with answering gaze, another's eyes,
And so are changed that they appear in guise 5
  Of two desires, to weep and prove my woe;
  And often they so mourn that Love doth
    show
Round them the circles of my miseries.

SONNET XXIX

From *V. N.* c. 40. The spell of the enchantress was, however, broken. A vision, as he records, in which he saw at noonday the form of Beatrice arrayed in crimson, as he had seen her in the days of her childhood, probably one of those referred to in *Purg.* xxx. 134, recalled him to his first love. His eyes, as in *Conv.* iii. 9, are inflamed with weeping. In the Italian we have, in ll. 5 and 8, the suggestive rhymes *desiri* and *martiri*, as in *B.* iii. 8, 10; *S.* xxviii. 11, 14.

These thoughts and sighs I breathe into the air
Grow in my heart so full of grief and pain 10
That Love grows faint as death for very woe;
Wherefore in their deep sorrow they complain,
And have my Lady's sweet name written there,
And many words that from her death do flow.

SONNET XXX

PILGRIMS IN FLORENCE

Deh peregrini, che pensosi andate

Ye pilgrims, who pass on with thoughtful mien,
Musing, perchance, of things now far away,
Take ye from such a distant land your way,
As one may judge from what in you is seen?

SONNET XXX.

From *V. N.* c. 41. Pilgrims were seen in the streets of Florence on their way to Rome to see the *sudarium* of St. Veronica, the *vera icon* of the face of Christ, which was exhibited annually at St. Peter's. See *Par.* xxxi. 104, *n.* With a subtle power, which we may almost call Shakespearean or Browning-like, Dante thinks how little he can think their thoughts, how little they can think his. Comp. *Purg.* viii. 1–9. We are reminded of the threefold "I think he thought that I thought" of *H.* xiii. 25. They pass by Beatrice's house, and little dream of all the memories of joys and sorrows that it has for him. What if he should tell them that Florence has lost her Beatrice, her blessedness, and that one, at least, still weeps for that loss? If we connect this exhibition of the Veronica with the Jubilee, of which it was one of the chief attractions, this would bring the close of the *Vita Nuova* to about the beginning of A.D. 1300, and so would form a link with the assumed date of the opening of the *Inferno*. There is no reason, however, to think that the Veronica was not shown at certain seasons every year. L. 6 gives us in *la città dolente* a link with *H.* i. 1.

For ye weep not, as ye pass on between 5
The woeful city's streets in sad array,
As they might do whose careless looks display
That they know nought of all her anguish keen.
But if ye will remain with wish to hear,
My heart tells me in sooth with many a sigh, 10
That, as ye leave it, ye will surely weep:
She hath beheld her Beatricè die,
And what a man may wish to say of her,
Hath power the hearer's eyes in tears to steep.

SONNET XXXI

BEATRICE TRANSFIGURED

Oltre la spera, che più larga gira

Beyond the sphere that wheeleth widest round
Passeth the sigh that issues from my heart;
New power of mind, that Love's might doth impart
With tears to it, draws it to higher ground.

SONNET XXXI

From *V. N.* c. 42, and the last poem in it. We are drawing near the threshold of the definite resolve, after yet another vision (the germ of that with which the *Commedia* opens?), that he would say of Beatrice what had never yet been said of woman. The Sonnet, we are told, was written at the request of two noble ladies who admired his poems, and asked him to write something new for them. He accordingly wrote what follows, and sent it to them with *Sonnets* xxiii. and xxx.

1 The "sphere" is the *primum mobile*, which includes all the eight spheres of mediæval astronomy. Beyond it is the Empyrean Heaven, the abode of God. There is the "goal of all desire," and

When it the goal of all desire hath found, 5
It sees a lady clothed with honour bright,
And shineth so, that through that glorious light
Clear visions for the pilgrim soul abound.
It sees her such that when its tale it tells,
I hear it not, it speaks so soft and low 10
To the sad heart that bids it speak of her;
Yet that it speaks of that fair dame I know,
Since on my Beatricè oft it dwells,
So that I hear it well, O ladies dear.

CANZONE VIII

PAIN OF SEPARATION

Amor, dacchè convien pur ch' io mi doglia

Love, since 'tis meet that I should tell my woe,
That men may list to me,
And show myself with all my manhood gone,
Grant that I may content in weeping know;
So that my grief set free 5

there is Beatrice (*Conv.* ii. 4). The "pilgrim soul" of l. 10 seems to present a link with *S.* xxx.

CANZONE VIII

A great gap divides the poems of the *Vita Nuova* from those that follow, and date, meaning, occasion, become more and more (if that, indeed, be possible, looking to the wanderings of interpreters, even within that region) matters of conjecture. Often there is but scanty evidence of authorship. In the present instance we have two *data* connecting the *Canzone* with Dante's life. It was written when he

My words may utter, with my sense at one.
Thou will'st my death, and I consent
thereon;
But who will pardon if I lack the art
To tell my pain of heart?
Who will believe what now doth me con-
strain? 10
But if from thee fit words for grief are won,
Grant, O my Lord, that, ere my life depart,
That cruel fair one may not hear my pain,
For, of my inward grief were she made ware,
Sorrow would make her beauteous face less
fair. 15

was in exile (l. 78). It was a song of the mountains (61, 76), in the valley of the river on whose banks he had felt the power of love. All this points to the upper valley of the Arno, the Casentino district, which is described in *H.* xxx. 65, and *Purg.* v. 94, xiv. 43, and in which he found a temporary home with Alessandro da Romena during his wanderings. A letter which Witte has brought to light (*Frat. O. M.* iii. 430) is probably connected with it. Dante writes *circ.* 1309 from the Casentino to the Marquis Moroello Malaspina of the Lunigiana, to whom he is said to have dedicated his *Purgatorio.* He dwells on the fact that in that region he had found a lady whose manners and character had attracted him. Of her rank or parentage or fortune we know nothing. He says that he sends a poem with the letter which will explain his feelings more fully. This *Canzone* is conjecturally identified with that poem, and that would give *circ.* 1309 as its date. One does not read it with any great satisfaction. I assume that a man like Dante would not write to tell a friend and patron like Moroello of the progress of a criminal intrigue, and that the attachment was therefore of the platonic type. On the other hand, Dante was now forty-four, and the sighs and piled-up agonies which were real at twenty seem at that age somewhat artificial. Even the platonic attachment seems to involve something like unfaithfulness to the memory of Beatrice, *after* the ideal conversion of 1300, and while he was actually writing the *Purgatorio,* as well as to poor Gemma, who was left in Florence. On the other hand, one should remember that Italian nature is not English; that Dante's loneliness of exile might well create a passionate longing for sympathy; that when he found one whose presence seemed to brighten the gloom of life, his thoughts would run naturally in the old grooves and find utterance after the old form. There would be a certain satisfaction in feeling that the fountains which had once flowed so freely were not dried up, even though there was more effort in drawing the buckets from the well. I do not care to submit the water so drawn to a minute analysis. Some allowance must be made, I believe, in

I cannot 'scape from her, but she will come
Within my phantasy,
More than I can the thought that brings her there:
The frenzied soul that brings its own ill home,
Painting her faithfully, 20
Lovely and stern, its own doom doth prepare:
Then looks on her, and when it filled doth fare
With the great longing springing from mine eyes,
Wroth with itself doth rise,
That lit the fire where it, poor soul! doth burn. 25
What plea of reason calms the stormy air
When such a tempest whirls o'er inward skies?
The grief it cannot hold breaks forth in sighs,
From out my lips that others too may learn,
And gives mine eyes the tears they truly earn. 30

The image of my fair foe which doth stay
Victorious and proud,
And lords it o'er my faculty of will,
Desirous of itself, doth make me stray
There, where its truth is showed, 35
As like to like its course directing still.

that process for the allegorising tendency. The haughtiness and coldness of the Casentinese lady would remind such a thinker as Dante of what had been said of Wisdom herself; that she at first is found unpleasant to the unlearned (*Ecclus.* vi. 20–28; *Conv.* iii. 15), and reserves the joy of her countenance for those who seek her with a persevering love.

Like snow that seeks the sun, so fare I ill;
But I am powerless, and I am as they
Who thither take their way
As others bid, where they must fall as dead. 40
When I draw near, a voice mine ears doth fill,
Which saith: "Away! seek'st thou his death to see?"
Then look I out, and search to whom to flee
For succour:—to this pass I now am led
By those bright eyes that baleful lustre shed. 45

What I become when smitten, thus, O Love,
Thou can'st relate, not I;
For thou dost stay to look while I lie dead,
And if my soul back to my heart should move,
Blind loss of memory 50
Hath been with her while she from earth hath fled.
When I rise up, and see the wound that bled,
And cast me down sore smitten by the blow,
No comfort can I know,
To keep me from the shuddering thrill of fear; 55
And then my looks, with pallor o'er them spread,
Show what that lightning was that laid me low.
For, grant it came with sweet smile all aglow,
Long time all clouded doth my face appear,
Because my spirit gains no safety clear. 60

Thus thou hast brought me, Love, to Alpine vale,
Where flows the river bright,
Along whose banks thou still o'er me dost reign.
Alive or dead thou dost at will assail,
Thanks to the fierce keen light, 65
Which flashing opes the way for Death's campaign.
Alas! for ladies fair I look in vain,
Or kindly men, to pity my deep woe.
If she unheeding go,
I have no hope that others help will send. 70
And she, no longer bound to thy domain,
Cares not, O Sire, for dart that thou dost throw;
Such shield of pride around her breast doth go,
That every dart thereon its course doth end;
And thus her heart against them doth defend. 75

Dear mountain song of mine, thou goest thy way,
Perchance thou'lt Florence see, mine own dear land,
That drives me doomed and banned,
Showing no pity, and devoid of love.
If thou dost enter there, pass on, and say, 80
"My lord no more against you can wage war,
There, whence I come, his chains so heavy are,
That, though thy fierce wrath placable should prove,
No longer freedom hath he thence to move."

61 I have given above what seems the true explanation of the words. Local ambitions have, however, led some Italian scholars to identify the Alps with the mountains of the Lago di Garda, and the river with the Adige. (Comp. *H.* xii. 5.)

CANZONE IX

THE LOVER'S THREATS

Così nel mio parlar voglio esser aspro

FAIN in my speech would I be harsh and rough,
As is in all her acts that rock so fair,
Which hourly comes to share
More hardness, and less penetrable stuff,
And clothes itself all o'er with jasper bright, [5]
So that, as stopped by it or halting there,
No arrow forth doth fare,

CANZONE IX

I own that I insert this *Canzone* with grave misgivings as to its authorship. It is true that it appears in all printed editions, is found with Dante's name in many MSS., and is accepted by experts like Fraticelli and Witte. On the other hand, I fail to find in it the grace, the subtlety, the pathos of the heart and hand of Dante. The threats of ll. 67–79, have a wild sensual Swinburnian eagerness of passion in them, of which we find no trace in Dante's other writings. I am disposed to couple it with another poem, an auctioneer's inventory of beauties, dealing largely with "blond and curled locks" "*Io miro i crespi e gli biondi capelli*," which was at one time, at Venice in 1508, printed as Dante's, and out of which an Italian scholar (Missirini) constructed an ideal portrait of Beatrice, but which is now generally assigned to Fazio degli Uberti, or some other second or third class poet. Witte, it may be noted, is disposed to find an allegorical meaning, like that which pervades the poetry of the Persian mystics and the mediæval interpretation of the *Song of Solomon*, in the threats of which I have spoken, and in which he sees the struggles of the intellect to attain the fruition of truth by its own persistent efforts—efforts which the seeker afterwards renounced for the submission of faith and hope. On the assumption of a literal meaning, commentators, seeing that a reference to Beatrice is out of the question, have identified the fair one to whom the *Canzone* is addressed with the Gentucca of *Purg.* xxiv. 38, or the Casentino lady of the *Ep.* to Moroello Malaspina, or to a Pietra de' Scrovigni of Padua, the last conjecture resting on the paronomasia of l. 2.

The allusion to Dido (l. 37) is almost the one point of contact with anything that we know of Dante's thoughts and studies (*H.* v. 85), but it is scarcely conclusive as evidence of authorship.

That ever on unsheltered part doth light:
And shield and hauberk fail when she doth
 smite,
Nor can a man escape those deadly blows, 10
 Which come upon her foes,
As if with wings, and crush each strong defence;
So to resist her I make no pretence.

I find no shield that she cannot break through,
No place that hides me from her piercing
 eyes; 15
 But as o'er spray doth rise
The blossom, so my mind with her is crowned;
She seems as much to care for all my woe,
As ship for sea that calm and waveless lies;
 My deep-sunk grief defies 20
All power of utterance that in rhymes is
 bound.
Ah, cruel pain, that, like sharp file, hast
 ground,
So silently, my strength of life away,
 Why hast thou no dismay
Thus to devour my whole heart, bit by bit, 25
As I to tell who gives thee strength for it.

For more my heart doth tremble, musing much
Of her, where I meet gaze of other eyes,
 For fear lest no disguise 30
Should keep my thoughts from being by look
 betrayed,
Than I from death do shrink, when he, with
 touch
Of Love's sharp teeth, doth every sense
 surprise:
 Whence weak and prostrate lies

My mind's whole strength, all dull and
 laggard made.
Low hath he smitten me now, and hath
 displayed
The sword that Dido slew all ruthlessly,
 E'en Love, to whom I cry,
Calling for mercy in my lowly prayer;
And he denies, and leaves me to despair.

Once and again he lifts his hand to smite,
That cruel Lord, and all hope passeth by;
 So that I prostrate lie
Upon the earth, of power to stir bereft.
Then in my mind new troubles rise in might,
And all the blood, which through my veins
 doth fly,
 As hearing my heart's cry,
Flows thitherward, and thus I pale am left.
And on the left side I by him am cleft,
So sorely that my whole heart throbs with
 pain.
 Then say I, "Once again
Should he lift hand, Death will have gained
 his prey
Before the fatal blow descends to slay."

Had I thus seen him cleave the heart in twain
Of that harsh Fair who cleaves my heart in
 four
 Death would be dark no more,
To whom I pass for her great beauty's sake.
For in the sun as well as in the rain
That ruthless deadly fair her scorn doth
 pour.
 Ah, why wails she no more

For me, as I for her in fiery lake?
For soon I'd cry, "I will not thee forsake."
Gladly I'd do it, as though he I were
Who, in those ringlets fair,
Which Love for my undoing crisps with gold, 65
Should plunge his hand, and revel in their hold.

And if I had those tresses in my hand,
Which are as rod or scourge that makes me mourn,
I would grasp them at morn,
And hold them till the bells of evensong. 70
Nor would I piteous be, nor gently bland,
But, like a bear at play, act out my scorn;
And if by Love's scourge torn,
For vengeance thousand-fold should I be strong;
And on her bright eyes, whence the flashes throng 75
That set on fire the heart I bear half-slain,
I would my fixed glance strain,
To 'venge me for the flight that wrought my pain,
And then with Love would grant her peace again.

Canzon', go straight to that my Lady fair 80
Who hath my heart so pierced, and takes by wrong
That for which most I long;
And with thine arrow at her proud heart aim,
For in such vengeance win we chiefest fame.

SONNET XXXII

THE LOVER'S ANATHEMA

Io maledico il dì ch' io vidi in prima

I CURSE the day when first I saw the light
  Of thy bright eyes so treacherously fair,
  The hour when thou didst come upon the
      height
Of this my heart to call my soul elsewhere;   5
Love's filing tool with curse I also smite,
  Which smoothed my songs, and colours rich
      and rare,
  That I have found for thee, and rhymed
      aright,
So that the world to thee its praise might bear.
And I curse too my memory hard as steel,
  So firm to keep what bringeth death to me,   10
That is, thy looks which grace and guilt reveal,
  Through which Love oft is led to perjury;
So that at him and me men's laugh rings free,
As though I would rob Fortune of her wheel.

SONNET XXXII

In some early collections the Sonnet appears with the name of Cino da Pistoia, to whom I am myself disposed to assign it. If Dante's, it must be referred to some pang of disappointment at the rejection of his affection by the lady of the Casentino or Pietra de' Scrovigni. See *Canz.* viii. and ix. I scarcely see how an allegorical meaning can be read between the lines. An anathema on the earthly philosophy which he was leaving for a higher wisdom is perhaps conceivable, but is not, I think, probable.

[8] The words present an almost verbal coincidence with *S.* xlii. 1. For the "wheel of fortune" see *H.* vii. 96.

BALLATA VI

IGNORANCE IN ASKING

Donne, io non so di che mi preghi Amore

LADIES, I know not what of Love to pray,
  For he smites me, and death is hard to bear,
  And yet to feel him less brings greater fear.

There shineth in the centre of my mind
  The light of those fair eyes that I desire, 6
    Which gives my soul content;
True is it that at times a dart I find
  Which drieth up my heart's well as with fire,
    Ere all its force be spent;
This doeth Love as oft as he doth paint 10
  That gentle hand and that pure faithfulness,
  Which should my life with sense of safety
      bless.

BALLATA VI

Authorship, date, and occasion uncertain. The address to "Ladies" reminds us of some of the poems of the Beatrice period (*Canz.* ii. 1; *S.* xii. 1, xiv. 1). Line 8 finds a parallel in *H.* i. 20.

BALLATA VII

MEMORIES

Madonna, quel signor, che voi portate

LADY, the sovran Lord thou so dost bear
In thy bright eyes, that he subdues all power,
Of surety gives me dower,
That thou with pity wilt full friendship share;

For there, where he doth find his home and bower 5
And has society so passing fair,
He draws what's good and rare
To him, as to the fountain-head of power.
Hence I find comfort for my hope, full store,
Which hath so long been rent and tempest tost, 10
That it had sure been lost,
Had it not been that Love
Against all adverse fortune help doth prove,
With his bare look and with remembered lore
Of the sweet spot and of the flowery grove, 15
Which, with new hues, all hues of earth above,
Encircleth all my mind and memory,
Thanks to thy sweet and gracious courtesy.

BALLATA VII

What has been said of *B.* vi. holds good of this also. Line 1 reads like a reproduction of *S.* xi. 1. It may have been one of the many "*cosette*" (*V. N.* c. 5) which he wrote for the "screen" lady between 1283 and 1285, of which Beatrice was the subject, but which he did not care to include in the *V. N.* Line 15 seems to find an echo in the vision of the Earthly Paradise (*Purg.* xxviii. 1-36).

BALLATA VIII

THE GARLAND

Per una ghirlandetta

By reason of a garland fair
That once I saw, each single flower
Now makes me breathe a sigh.

I saw thee, Lady, bear that garland fair,
Sweetest of flowers that blow, 5
And over it, as floating in the air
I saw Love's angel hover meek and low,
And in his song's sweet flow,
He said, "Who looks on me
Will praise my Lord on high." 10

Should I be haply where a floweret blows,
A sigh must I suspire,
And say, "Where'er my gentle lady goes,
Her brow doth bear the flowerets of my Sire:
But to increase desire, 15
My Lady sure will be
Crowned by Love's majesty.

BALLATA VIII

I incline to think that this also was addressed to Beatrice. Her lover sees her adorned with a wreath of flowers (comp. *Purg.* xxx. 28), crowned as by the Lord of love, and over her hovers the angel of love and lowliness.

My slender words a tale of flowers have told
    In ballad quaint and new;
And for their brightness they a garment fold, 20
    Not such as others knew.
    Therefore I pray to you,
    That, when one sings it, ye
    Should show it courtesy.

SONNET XXXIII

LOVE'S SOVEREIGNTY

Io sono stato con Amore insieme

I HAVE with Love in contact close been thrown,
  From the ninth year the sun did mark for me,
  And know how he now curb, now spur may
    be,
And how beneath him men may smile and groan.

SONNET XXXIII

Here we stand on somewhat surer ground. A Sonnet is extant written by Cino da Pistoia to Dante, asking whether one who had loved truly and passionately could ever come under the power of a like love again. To that question this Sonnet is the affirmative answer. It maintains that love comes on us, mastering our free-will, and leaving us no choice but to obey, and so far agrees in tone with the letter about the Casentino lady (*Ep.* 3) before referred to. It may be, as Fraticelli conjectures, the Sonnet alluded to in the letter, "*exulanti Pistoriensi*" (probably Cino), dealing with the same question (*Frat. O. M.* iii. 434). Cecco d' Ascoli refers to it, quoting the first line in his *Acerba*, iii. 1. Neither Krafft nor Witte, it may be noted, admits it in the editions they have severally published.

[1] For the fact see *V. N.* c. 1; for the form of statement, *Conv.* ii. 7.

Who strives with him, with skill and strength
alone, 5
Acts as he does who, when the storm plays
free,
Rings out a peal, as though the vaporous sea
And thunderous strife that music could atone.
Wherefore within the range of that his bow,
Free choice to act hath not its freedom true, 10
So that our counsels vain dart to and fro.
Well with new spur in flank may he us
prick,
And each new pleasure he before us lays,
We must needs follow, of the old joy sick.

6 The words probably refer to the practice of ringing church bells during a thunderstorm. That, Dante says, in its impotence to stop the tempest, is like the powerlessness of the will when the storms of passion are rolling over it. It is his *apologia*, afterwards, we may believe, recanted (*Purg.* xxxi. 31-66), for the passing affections that obscured the memory of Beatrice. Here also, of course, an allegorical meaning is conceivable. For the custom see Brand's *Popular Antiquities*, ii. 217, 218; *ed.* 1875.

PART II

SONNET XXXIV

THE ENVOY'S INSTRUCTIONS

Parole mie, che per lo mondo siete

YE words of mine, whose voice the world doth
fill,
Who had your birth when first my thoughts
began
To speak of her for whom astray I ran;
"*Ye, who the third heaven move, by force of will,*"
Knowing her well, to her your course fulfil, 5
So wailing that she may our sorrows scan:
Say to her, "We are thine, nor think we can
Present ourselves henceforth more numerous
still."

SONNET XXXIV

The quotation in line 4 of *Canz.* xiv. 1 is conclusive as to authorship. The opening lines imply a consciousness of fame already widely spread, resting on the older sister poems of the *V. N.* The line quoted in line 4 is from the first of those explained allegorically in the *Convito.* The fact that it thus belongs to the second stage of Dante's Trilogy, of which the *Convito* is the embodiment, justifies its place as the opening of Part ii. Line 3 implies, as I render "*in cui errai*" (the words have been taken, however, as "against whom I sinned"), an admission that he had sinned in thought, in not remembering the Divine Wisdom of which Beatrice had become the symbol. He bids these poems of Part ii., now collected, go to the Philosophy, who, as the ideal object of his second love, is the subject of the *Convito*, and tells her that their number is complete. They cannot, however, hope to find in her

Stay not with her; for Love is not found there,
  But take your way around in sad array, 10
Like your own sisters in the days that were.
And when ye find a lady kind and fair,
  Right humbly at her feet your tribute lay,
And say, "To thee we gifts of honour bear."

SONNET XXXV

FOR OTHERS' SAKE

Chi guarderà giammai senza paura

WHO now will ever look devoid of fear
  Into this fair and tender maiden's eyes,
  Which so have wrought on me that now
    there lies
Before me nought but death, to me so drear?

reciprocity of affection, for she is passionless in her beauty. The Sonnet seems like a kind of *apologia* for the endeavour to combine the new teachings of Philosophy with the old reverence for Beatrice, an *apologia* of which *Purg.* xxx. 100–145 may be looked on as a recantation. The "sisters" are probably the poems of the *V. N.* The "lady kind and fair" (*donna di valore*) is identified in *Conv.* iii. 14 with any noble soul that sympathises with the pursuit of wisdom.

SONNET XXXV

The allegorical sense is again dominant. He had loved the "fair maid" of whom he speaks (his use of the word "*pargoletta*" suggests that that term in *Purg.* xxxi. 59 has both a literal and a symbolic meaning) not wisely but too well. His long pursuit of philosophy had been exhausting and unsatisfying. His strength is failing, life seems waning. Let others take warning by his example, lest the attractions of her bright eyes, *i.e.*, as in *Conv.* iii. 15, the demonstrations of Philosophy, draw them to a like peril of death. True life, he seems to say, is not found in that path. L. 10 seems an echo of *John* xi. 50.

See how my evil fortune is severe; 5
For from all lives, my life the destinies
Chose as the type of perilous emprise,
That none to gaze on that fair face draw near.
To me this end was given by Fortune's might;
Since it must needs be that one man should
die, 10
That others to that peril come not nigh.
Therefore, alas! thus drawn along was I,
Attracting to me my life's opposite,
As doth the pearl the star of day's clear light.

BALLATA IX

TERRIBLE IN BEAUTY

Io mi son pargoletta bella e nuova

"A MAIDEN young and beautiful am I,
And I am come that I may show to you
The beauties of the region where I grew:

[14] The pearl was supposed to be formed by the power of the sun, but if it was imperfect, it could not receive that power (*Conv.* iv. 20).

BALLATA IX

The reappearance of "*pargoletta*" in line 1 leads to the conclusion that she who speaks, manifesting what she is without speaking, is neither the living nor the transfigured Beatrice, but the Philosophy whom, in the *Convito* stage of his inner life, he had admittted to a co-ordinate share in his affections, not without the risk of its becoming predominant. So taken, Philosophy boasts, as in *Conv.* ii. 16, of her heavenly origin. To that heaven she will return to give a fresh joy to its inhabitants. The poet then transfers to her what he had written of old of Beatrice herself. To assume, with Fraticelli,

I come from Heaven, and thither shall return,
  To give to others joy in my clear light: 5
And he who sees me, nor with love doth burn,
  Of love shall never have clear-visioned sight:
  For nothing was denied to my delight,
When Nature begged me of him as her due,
Who wills, dear ladies, me to join with you. 10

Each star that shines within mine eye doth rain
  Showers of its light, and of its potency:
My beauties to the world as new remain,
  Because from Heaven's high clime they come
    to me;
  Nor can men ever know them perfectly, 15
Save by the knowledge of a man in whom
Love dwells, with joy all others to illume."

These words are read as written in the eye
  Of a bright angel, seen with beauty rife,
Whence I who, to escape, looked steadfastly, 20
  Incur the risk of forfeiting my life;
  For such a wound I met in that fierce strife
From one whom I within her eyes beheld,
That I go weeping, all my peace dispelled.

that the "*pargoletta*" is Beatrice, seems to me at variance with *Purg*. xxxi. 59, as interpreting the successive stages of Dante's inner life, to say nothing of the fact that the term could hardly be applied to one who, like Beatrice, was a "*donna*."

11 Each planet had its own special influence, presided over its own special study in the *Trivium* and *Quadrivium* (*Conv*. ii. 14). All were found combined in Philosophy, as the Queen of Sciences. To understand their preciousness required the love which shows itself in self-renunciation.

19 The "angel" is clearly the "maiden" of line 1, *i.e.*, Philosophy. In gazing on her in the hope of an escape of some sort, we have a reproduction of the thought of *V. N.* c. 36, when he had found in the "gentle lady" of the window, a refuge from over-much sorrow. As it was, however, his devotion to that new affection, to the service of the new mistress, Philosophy, had brought with it a new suffering, and he was well nigh sick unto death. I do not see any adequate

SONNET XXXVI

BEAUTIFUL AND PITILESS

E' non è legno di sì forti nocchi

No tree there is so gnarled and stiff to ply,
No rock that flinty hardness so doth fill,
But that the cruel fair who doth me kill
Can kindle love there with her beauteous eye.
Hence when one gazes as she passeth by, 5
If he withdraw not, Death will work his will,
So fails his heart; for vainly prays he still
That his stern office he may modify.
Ah! wherefore was such wondrous power
assigned
To the fair eyes of lady so severe, 10
Who careth not to save her worshipper,
And in such ruthless mood doth persevere,
That if one dies for her, to that she's blind,
And hides her beauties that he may not find?

grounds for finding the "*pargoletta*" in either Gentucca or the lady of the Casentino.

SONNET XXXVI

The "stern lady" whose eyes have such terrible power is, as in *S.* xxxv., *B.* ix., Philosophy. Having once started the idea that this was the "gentle lady" who had pity on him (*V. N.* c. 38; *Conv.* ii. 2), he plays with it, presents it in many aspects, writes poems which half veil and half reveal his meaning, φωνᾶντα συνετοῖσιν—words for the wise, puzzles for the Philistines—not without a certain pleasure in the thought that they will mystify his readers.

Conv. ii. 1 explains the "stocks" and "stones" of men without art or knowledge. Even there Philosophy, with her Orphic power, moves to love; but the love is one of the δεινοὶ ἔρωτες, the "terrible passions" of which Plato speaks. She looks on at their fruitless efforts, sees them wither and perish in striving to obtain her, and yet she hides herself from them and they have no fruition.

The words "*si spanocchi*" in l. 8, literally to deal out the grains

SONNET XXXVII

A CRY FOR HELP

Se vedi gli occhi miei di pianger vaghi

If thou dost see mine eyes so fain to weep,
Through the new sorrow that devours my heart,
By her I pray, who ne'er from thee doth part,
That thou, Sire, them from their desire would'st keep;
That is, that thy right hand should vengeance heap 5
On him who murders justice, and doth flee
To tyrant lord, and sucks his poison free,
Wherewith he fain would all the wide world steep,

an ear of corn one by one, is, I think, sufficiently expressed by "modify." The judgment is to come bit by bit.

SONNET XXXVII

It is with a certain satisfaction that we come, in the midst of all the marvellous, half-morbid introspections of the Minor Poems, upon one which brings us face to face with the man of action, whose interests range widely over the kingdoms of the world. The Sonnet takes its place among the many cries of "How long, O Lord, how long?" which have gone up from the patriots and reformers of all countries, of none more than of Italy. The vague words, distinct enough to him who wrote them, leave us to guess to what special crisis of Dante's life they belong. The Sonnet may be addressed to the Emperor Henry VII. (comp. *Ep.* 5, vol. i. p. cv.), or, as I think more probable, to the great Emperor of the Universe. She who never parts from the earthly or the heavenly Emperor is the eternal justice of God. He who "murders Justice" may be the Neri party of Florence, or Charles of Valois, or Boniface VIII., or Philip the Fair of France; the "tyrant" may be, according as we adopt one or other of these hypotheses, Charles, or Boniface VIII., or Philip, or Clement V. The "poison" is the grasping greed of gain, for

And hath of so great terror cast the chill
Into thy subjects' hearts, that all are dumb: 10
But thou, Love's fire, whose light the Heaven doth fill,
Raise thou that Virtue who lies all o'ercome,
Naked and cold, and screen her with thy veil,
For without her, all peace on earth doth fail.

SONNET XXXVIII

DISAPPOINTMENT

Per quella via che la bellezza corre

Along the pathway Beauty loves to tread
When to awaken Love it seeks the mind,
There wends a lady, sportively inclined,
As one who deems that I by her am led,

which both Philip and Clement were conspicuous. I incline to the last of the four combinations (comp. *Purg.* xxxii. 151-160), and refer the Sonnet to the indignation with which Dante looked on the suppression of the Templars (*Purg.* xx. 93), to the hopes which he began to cherish after the election of Henry VII.

SONNET XXXVIII

The enigma deepens. Dark sayings become darker. We say, as the Jews did of Ezekiel, "Doth he not speak parables?" The key to the puzzle may be found, I believe, in the thought that the two ladies are Human and Divine Wisdom; that the tower is, in Bunyan's language, that of Man-soul; that the path by which beauty passes into the heart is that of sight; that the gate is that of the will. I see in the Sonnet a kind of palinode of the praises lavished on Philosophy in the *Convito*; a recognition that a true Theology has, after all, higher claims, a transition to the spirit of the *Purgatory* and *Paradise.* The "gentle lady" must, after all, give way to Beatrice. The poet returns to his first love. See *Study on the Genesis and Growth of the Commedia*, vol. v.

And when she comes where soars the high
tower's head, 5
Which opens when the soul consent doth find,
She hears a voice come floating swift as wind,
" Rise, Lady fair, nor enter there," it said.
For to that Lady who doth sit on high,
When she the sceptre of high lordship claimed, 10
Love granted it, according to her will.
And when that fair one sees herself passed by,
Driven from that mansion which Love's home
is named,
She back returns and shame her face doth fill.

SONNET XXXIX

STELLAR INFLUENCES

Da quella luce, che il suo corso gira

From that bright star which moveth on its way
For ever at the Empyrean's will,
And between Mars and Saturn ruleth still,
E'en as the expert astrologer doth say,

SONNET XXXIX

We are still in the region of allegory. The Sonnet is a condensed expression of the theory of planetary influence and correspondences, stated at length in *Conv.* ii. 14 (comp. *Ball.* ix. 11; *Canz.* 14), where the seven spheres are placed over against the seven studies of the *Trivium* (Grammar, Dialectic, Rhetoric) and the *Quadrivium* (Arithmetic, Music, Geometry, and Astronomy). The sphere of the fixed stars corresponds in like manner to Physics and Metaphysics; the *Primum Mobile* to Ethics; the Empyrean to Theology. We are left to guess whether the poet speaks of Beatrice or the "*donna gentile*," of Theology or Philosophy, and

She, who inspires me with her beauty's ray, 5
Doth subtle art of sovereignty distil;
And he whose glory doth the fourth heaven fill,
Gives her the power my longing soul to sway;
And that fair planet known as Mercury
Colours her speech with all its virtue rare; 10
And the first heaven its boon does not deny;
She who the third heaven ruleth as her share,
Makes her heart full of utterance pure and free:
So all the seven to perfect her agree.

BALLATA X

THE SCORN OF SCORN

Voi che sapete ragionar d' amore

Ye who are skilled of Love discourse to hold,
Hear ye this ballad-song of mine forlorn,
Which telleth of a lady full of scorn,
Who, through her power, my whole heart hath
controlled.

the answer to that question must depend on the date which we assign to the Sonnet. Assuming that it rightly follows *S.* xxxviii., I incline to the former view. The systematic arrangement of the *Paradise*, according to the ten heavenly spheres, falls in with this interpretation.

[1] Jupiter lies between Mars and Saturn; the sun, in the Ptolemaic system, is in the fourth heaven (l. 7); the first heaven (l. 11) is that of the moon; the third (l. 12) that of Venus, which represents the persuasive power of rhetoric. Comp. *Canz.* xiv.

BALLATA X.

Here the writer explains his own enigmas. He tells us (*Conv.* iii. 9–15) that he wrote this *Ballata* to represent the aspect which

So doth she scorn whoe'er on her doth gaze, 5
She makes him bend his eyes for very fear,
For still round hers she evermore displays
A portraiture of cruelty severe;
While yet within the image sweet they bear
Which makes the gentle soul speak thankful
praise; 10
So full of might that when 'tis seen, always
From every heart it draws forth sighs untold.

She seems to say, "I will not lowly be
Toward any one who gazeth on mine eyes;
For there I bear that Lord of courtesy 15
Whose darts have made new feelings in me rise."
And, certes, I believe she in such wise
Keeps them, to gaze upon them as she please:
E'en so an upright lady acts, who sees
How those who would do honour her behold. 20

I have no hope that pity her will move
To deign on others to bestow a glance;
So proud a lady is she, she who Love
Shows in her eyes, so fair of countenance.
But let her hide and keep him, as may chance, 25
That such bliss I awhile should see no more;
Yet shall my longings have at last a power
Against the scorn of Love so proud and cold.

Philosophy presents to the man void of understanding, to the seeker who as yet is unworthy of her gracious smile, and quotes in *Canz.* xv., of which *Conv.* iii. is an exposition, the very epithets of "proud" and "ruthless" which he here applies to her. She will not be lowly towards one who looks too boldly into her eyes, and requires in her lover the temper of reverential awe. But within, for those who so seek her, she has an aspect full of grace, and so his desires will have strength to persevere in their quest in spite of her seeming harshness. I assign the poem, with little hesitation, to the transition period of Dante's life, represented by the *Convito*, and therefore identify the "Lady" of whom it speaks with Philosophy. We are reminded at once of *Ecclus.* iv. 16–18, and of the Janus-like face of Wisdom in the Giotto fresco at Assisi.

SESTINA I

SIMILITUDES OF LOVE

Al poco giorno, ed al gran cerchio d' ombra

To shortened days and circle wide of shade
I have now come, alas! and snow-clad hills,
When all bright hues grow pale upon the grass;
Yet my desire hath not yet lost its green,
And so is rooted in the flinty rock, 5
Which speaks and hears, as though it were a
lady.

SESTINA I.

We come upon three poems, obviously of the same period, of a different type. They belong in their outward form to a class of which the Provençal poets were fond, and Arnauld Daniel, for whom in *Purg.* xxvi. 116 Dante expresses a profound reverence, was the inventor, as perhaps of the *terza rima*, so also of the *sestina*, ringing its manifold changes, like those of a chime of bells, upon the six words which are chosen as a theme. The metre was used afterwards by Petrarch and other poets. It is obvious that such a form is in the highest degree artificial, but, as with the equally artificial alphabetic Psalms of the Hebrews, the "Lamentations" of Jeremiah, or the strophes and antistrophes of a Greek chorus, the power of the poet to master it becomes a triumph of his strength. The performance, from our standpoint, seems to belong to the acrobats of poetry, but that exercise, as a part of literary gymnastic, may become part of the training of the athlete. As such I conceive Dante tried it. It was in his nature, as in the instance of Lucan (*H.* xxv. 94) and Ovid (*H.* xxv. 97), to match his strength against the great masters of poetry precisely in the points where they were supposed to be pre-eminent, and it will be owned that here also he has succeeded. It may be noted that the laws of the *Sestina* allowed the use of homonyms, *sc.*, of words of the same form and sound but different sense (as, *e.g.*, here in the use of *colli*=necks=hills), a licence of which the translator finds it difficult to avail himself. Where, as in this instance, the form is more than the matter, it is scarcely necessary to track the sequence of thought line by line. What one wonders at is that, under such conditions, there is any sequence at all. Briefly I take it that here also the "lady" is Philosophy. *Sest.* i. opens with the winter of discontent in which her worshipper finds himself (ll. 1-6). He

So in like manner doth this fair young lady
Stand frozen, as the snow stands in the shade,
For she no more is moved than is the rock,
When the sweet season comes which warms the
 hills, 10
And makes them change from white to pleasant
 green,
Because it clothes them all with flowers and grass.

When on her brow she wears a wreath of grass,
From out our thoughts she drives each other lady,
Since mingle there the crisp gold and the green, 15
So well that Love comes there to seek their shade,
Who shuts me up amid the lowly hills,
More closely far than doth the flinty rock.

Her beauties have more power than any rock,
Her blow may not be healed by any grass; 20
For I have fled through valleys and o'er hills,
That I might freedom gain from this fair lady.
But 'gainst her face I seek in vain for shade,
In hill, or wall, or tree with foliage green.

Aforetime I have seen her clothed in green, 25
So beautiful, she might have warmed a rock
With that Love which I bear to her mere shade;
Whence in a meadow bright with greenest grass,
I wooed her, as a love-inspiring lady,
On all sides girt by highest-soaring hills. 30

would fain escape (ll. 21-24), but cannot. He sees her clothed in green, the hue of hope (l. 25), yet for him there is small chance that she will accept his love, though he would sleep on the rock and feed on the grass, *i.e.*, lead the life of a hermit, if only he might behold but the skirts of her garment (ll. 31-36), while she shines like a precious gem where the shadows fall darkest (ll. 37-39). It may be noted that this *Sestina* is twice quoted in the *V. E.* (ii. 10, 13), in the latter case as an example of the higher style which is fit for one "*aulice poetantem*." In l. 39 I read "*la*" instead of "*gli*."

But sooner shall the streams flow up the hills
Ere this fair growth of plant so fresh and green
Shall kindle, as is wont with gentle lady,
For me, who fain would sleep upon the rock,
All my life long, and wander, eating grass, 35
Only to see her garments give their shade.

Where'er the hills cast round their darkest shade,
Beneath the fresh green doth the fair young lady
Dispel it, like rock crystal in the grass.

SESTINA II

SIMILITUDES OF LOVE

Amor mi mena tal fiata all' ombra

Love leads me many times beneath the shade
Of ladies fair, whose necks are beauteous hills,
And whiter far than flower of any grass;
And one there cometh, clothed in robes of
green,
Who in my heart dwells, as strength dwells in
rock, 5
And among others seems as fairest lady.

SESTINA II

Philosophy appears, as before, clothed in green, and with a wreath of flowers on her head. He feels, as before, the too seemingly incompatible impressions of her rigour and her sweetness (ll. 7–18). Of one thing he is certain, that his love for her makes him more lowly towards all others who, in any measure, reproduce her likeness. Never was any gem *intaglio* or painter's ideal of

And when I glance upon this gentle lady,
Whose brightness scatters every dusky shade,
Her light so smites my heart it turns to rock;
I roam, as strangled, all among the hills, 10
Till I revive, and am with love more green
Then ever yet was spring or freshest grass.

I ween no virtue ever was in grass
With power to heal, as dwells in this fair lady,
Who takes my heart, yet leaves my life all
green. 15
When she restores it, I am as a shade:
No longer have I life, save as the hills,
Which loftiest are, and of the hardest rock.

A heart I had as hard as any rock,
When I saw her as fresh as is the grass 20
In the sweet spring that clothes with flowers
the hills;
And now 'tis lowly found toward each fair lady:
Only through love of her who gives a shade
More precious than did ever foliage green.

For seasons hot or cold, or sere or green, 25
Still make me glad, to such sweet rest doth
rock
The great delight of resting in her shade.
O sight! how fair, to see her on the grass
Tripping more deftly than each other lady,
Dancing her way through valleys and o'er hills. 30

beauty so fair in its perfection as even the very shadow of her gracious loveliness (ll. 34-36). Neither this *Sestina* nor the following appears in the editions of Krafft and Witte, but Fraticelli gives what seem to me adequate reasons for receiving them.

Long as I dwell 'mid mountains and 'mid hills,
Love leaves me not, but keeps me fresh and
green,
As none he yet has kept for fairest lady;
For never yet was graving seen on rock,
Nor any form of colour fair on grass, 35
Which might seem bright as is her very shade.

Thus Love contents me, while I live in shade,
To find my joy and bliss in this fair lady,
Who on her head hath placed a wreath of
grass.

SESTINA III

SIMILITUDES OF LOVE

Gran nobiltà mi par vedere all' ombra

I SEEM to see great glory in the shade
Of ladies fair whose necks are ivory hills,
And each on other, as she goes, flings grass;
For she is there, through whom my life is
green,
And in her love fixed, as in wall a rock, 5
And stronger than was ever love for lady.

SESTINA III

The *tour de force* continues, as if the writer could go on for ever with variations upon the same theme. I do not find that the variations in this instance present any new features calling for special annotation.

If I have heart-love for mine own dear lady,
Let no man marvel, nor thereon cast shade;
For my heart, through her, holds its joy like
rock,
Which, were it not so, would bring low the
hills, 10
And so would change them as the hue of
green
Fades from the aspect of the new-mown
grass.

I well may say that she adorns the grass,
Which for adornment every other lady
Blends with fair flowers and foliage fresh and
green; 15
Because so brightly shineth her sweet shade,
That it makes glad the valleys, plains, and
hills,
And, certes, gives a virtue to the rock.

I know that I should be more vile than rock,
If she were not to me as healing grass: 20
She hath attained to scale the highest hills,
Which have been mounted by no other lady,
Save her alone, whom I love in the shade,
Like little bird half-hid in foliage green.

And if I were like lowly plant and green, 25
I could disclose the virtue of each rock,
And none should hide itself beneath the
shade;
For I am hers, her flower, her fruit, her grass;
But none can do as doth my gentle lady,
Whether she cometh down, or climbs, the
hills. 30

I seem alway as one who climbs the hills,
When I part from her; and feel fresh and
green,
So do I joy, in looking on my lady:
And when I see her not, like any rock
I stand, and watch in faith, still fresh as grass, 35
That soul who finds her chief joy in the shade.

More I seek not, than ever in her shade
To stand, who is of all the noblest lady,
Fairer than any flowers, or leaves, or grass.

CANZONE X

HARD AS A ROCK

Amor, tu vedi ben, che questa donna

Love, thou see'st well that this my Lady fair
For thy great power cares not at any time,
Which rules as mistress over others fair:
And when she saw she was my Lady fair,
By that bright ray which on my face shed
light; 5
Of cruelty she grew the mistress fair,

CANZONE X

The form adopted, that of a double *sestina*, seems the *ne plus ultra* of fantastic complication. There are sixty-six lines, and to these five words only are allowed as rhymes, and the changes are rung on these with manifold iteration, till the reader is constrained to say, "Enough, and more than enough," It is almost useless in such a case to expect any subtle insight or profound emotion. It is

And seemed to have no heart of lady fair,
But of some creature wild, to love most cold:
For, through the season hot and through the
cold,
I see her semblance as a lady fair, 10
Who had been fashioned out of goodly rock,
By hand of one who best can grave the rock.

And I, who am more steadfast than a rock,
Obeying thee, through love of lady fair,
In secret bear the pressure of the rock 15
With which thou woundedst me, as 'twere a
rock,
That had annoyed thee for long length of
time;
So that it reached my heart where I am
rock.
And never was discovered any rock,
Which, from the sun's great power or its
own light, 20
Had in it so much virtue or such light,
Which could protect me from that self-same
rock,
So that it should not lead me with its cold
Thither, where I shall be as dead with cold.

simply, as before, a *tour de force*, as of one who can dance his hornpipe even in the heaviest fetters, exulting in the fact that he at least keeps time: that he can, even under this almost unendurable restraint, succeed in making the verses say what he meant them to say. It seems to me idle, in such a case, to draw biographical inferences and to identify the "*Pietra*" of the poem with a supposed Pietra de' Scrovigni of Padua as one of Dante's lady-loves (comp. *Cans.* 9, *n.*). So far as the poem expresses a real feeling, I refer it, as in the preceding poems, to Philosophy, as in the "*donna gentile*" of the second stage of the Trilogy of the poet's life.

20 The thought connects itself with the belief that precious stones, such as carbuncle, amethyst, heliotrope, or bloodstone (*H.* xxiv. 93), and the like, derived their special virtues directly from the sun.

Thou knowest, O Sire, that by the freezing
cold, 25
Water becomes a solid crystal rock,
Beneath the north-wind and its piercing
cold,
And aye the air, through elemental cold,
Is changed, that water, as a lady fair,
Reigns in that clime by reason of the cold. 30
So before look that seemeth icy cold,
Freezes my very blood full many a time,
And that same thought which shortens most
my time
Is all transformed into a humour cold,
Which, through mine eyes, doth find its way
to light, 35
There, where it first received that ruthless
light.

In her is met all beauty's varied light,
As also of all cruelty the cold
Runs to her heart, where dwelleth not thy
light;
Since in my eyes she shines with such a
light, 40
When I behold her, that her form in rock
I see, or wheresoe'er I turn my light.
And from her eyes there comes so sweet a
light,
That I care not for other ladies fair.
Would that she were more piteous Lady
fair 45
To me, who ask of her, in dark and light,
To serve her only in each place and time,
Nor for aught else desire to live long
time.

Wherefore, O Power, that art before all time,
  Before all motion and material light, 50
  Pity thou me, who pass such grievous time.
  Seek thou her heart now, for it is full time,
  So that through thee may vanish all the cold,
  Which lets me not, like others, live my time;
  For if there comes on me thy tempest time 55
  In this my state, that fair and goodly rock
  Will see me slain and sepulchred in rock,
  Never to rise again till past is Time,
  When I shall see if ever lady fair
  Was pitiless as is this Lady fair. 60

My Song, I bear in mind a Lady fair,
  Such that she is to me as flinty rock;
  Give thou me courage, where all men seem
      cold,
  So that I dare, in spite of all that cold,
  That new thing which thy form shall bring
      to light, 65
  Which never hath been done at any time.

65 We are reminded of Milton's "Things unattempted yet in prose or rhyme."

CANZONIERE

CANZONE XI

WINTER

Io son venuto al punto della rota

I to that point in the great wheel have come,
Wherein the horizon, when the sun doth set,
Brings forth the twin-starred heaven to our sight;
And Love's fair star away from us doth roam,
Through the bright rays obliquely on it met 5
In such wise that they veil its tender light;
That planet, which makes keen the cold of night,
Shows himself to us in the circle great,
Where each star of the seven casts little shade:
Yet lighter is not made 10
One single thought of Love, that, with its weight,
O'erloads my soul that is more hard than rock,
For its fast hold of image all of rock.

CANZONE XI

1-10 We note the display of astronomical knowledge as reminding us of numerous passages of the *Commedia* (*Purg.* ii. 1-6, ix. 1-9, xxv. 1-6, xxvii. 1-6, *et al.*). The fact to be stated is that it is winter, when the sun is in Capricorn, when therefore the opposite sign of the zodiac, the Gemini, rises as the sun is setting. Possibly the verses that follow describe phenomena that met in some given year, and if we could ascertain these (which, as yet, however, commentators have not succeeded in doing), we might be able to fix the date of the *Canzone* with absolute precision.

7 The planet is Saturn, the coldest of the planets, to the influence of which was traced the severity of an exceptionally hard

There riseth up from Ethiopia's sands
A wind from far-off clime which rends the air, 15
Through the sun's orb that heats it with its ray.
The sea it crosses; thence, o'er all the lands
Such clouds it brings that but for wind more fair,
O'er all our hemisphere 'twould hold its sway;
And then it breaks, and falls in whitest spray 20
Of frozen snow and pestilential showers,
Whence all the air is filled with wail and woe;
Yet Love who, when winds blow,
Draws up his net to heaven's eternal bowers,
Leaveth me not; so dear a lady fair 25
Is found that proud one, mine own Lady fair.

Fled far is every bird that loves the heat
From Europe's clime, where evermore are seen
The seven bright stars that are the lords of cold;
And others cease awhile their warblings sweet, 30
To sound no more until the Spring be green,
Unless their song by sorrow be controlled:
And all the creatures that are gay and bold

winter. I follow Krafft and Witte in thus interpreting. The phenomena of Nature might seem to wither all tender emotions, but the mind of the singer is still weighed down with the sad memories of a love unreciprocated.

14 The south wind blows, and brings with it clouds which discharge themselves in snow and rain, but still there is no change of feeling, for the beloved one is still obdurate. I look on the poem as describing, like its predecessors, the struggles of the seeker after wisdom, who woos Philosophy and feels that he woos in vain, as far as the full fruition of wisdom is concerned.

27 Many birds have fled from Europe, which never loses sight

By nature, are from Love emancipate,
Because the cold their spirits' strength doth kill: 35
Yet mine more Love doth fill;
For my sweet thoughts still keep their first estate,
Nor are they given me by the change of time;
My Lady gives them in her youth's brief time.

Now have the green leaves passed their fixèd bound, 40
Which the Ram's power to spring-tide life did stir,
To clothe the world; and all the grass is dead,
And each fair bough of verdure stript is found,
Unless it be in laurel, pine, or fir,
Or whatsoe'er its verdure doth not shed; 45
And now the season is so keen and dread,
It blights the flowerets on each wide champaign,
And ill by them the hoar-frost keen is borne;
Yet the sharp amorous thorn
Love from my heart will not draw out again, 50
For I to bear it still am strong alway,
Long as I live, though I should live alway.

of the Seven Stars of the North (Ursa Major; comp. *Purg*. i. 30, xxx. 1), to a warmer clime. Those that remain and all other living creatures feel the icy spell of winter and hybernate in silence, but love is still glowing in the soul, for it does not depend on the change of seasons, but on the might of its beloved one.

40 The leaves which spring (Aries, as in *H*. i. 38) had called forth are all, evergreens excepted, withered, but the lover's heart is still pricked with the thorn of sorrow, and will be so for ever.

The watery mists enshrouded pour their stream
From vapours that earth holds within her womb,
And sendeth upwards from the vasty deep; 55
And so the path on which the sun did gleam,
And gave me joy, a river is become,
And shall be long as winter sway doth keep.
Earth like a white enamelled form doth sleep;
And the still water turneth all to glass, 60
Through the sharp cold that binds it from afar:
Yet I from this my war
Have not turned back a single step to pass;
Nor will I turn; for, if the pain is sweet,
Death must surpass whatever else is sweet. 65

What then, my Canzon', will become of me
In the sweet spring-tide season when with showers
Love the wide earth from all the heavens shall fill:
When, in this freezing chill,
Love doth in me, not elsewhere, show his powers? 70
'Twill be the state of one as marble cold,
If maiden fair for heart hath marble cold.

53 The winter torrents rush down the watercourses that had been dry in summer, and the earth is frozen, but the warfare goes on. We note that the poet describes an Italian winter. The earth is frozen, but not the rivers or the lakes. The very pain of the conflict is sweet. How far sweeter will be death that ends it!

66 If this is the poet's state in winter, what will it be in spring, when love is stronger? If the beloved one still shows a heart of stone, the lover will be a stone also. As far as I know, the commentators who play the part of detectives have not found the Casentino lady or Gentucca in the "*pargoletta*" of the concluding lines, perhaps, as Witte says, through pure inattention. In the *Convito*, had it been completed, she would probably have appeared as Philosophy.

CANZONE XII

RETURN OF SPRING

Amor, che muovi tua virtù dal cielo

Love, who from Heaven thy virtue dost
unfold,
As the sun doth its light,
For there we learn most clearly what its
might,
Where its rays find the greatest nobleness;
And, as far off he drives the dark and
cold,
So thou, great Lord, enthronèd in the
height,
In others' hearts all vile thoughts putt'st to
flight,
Nor against thee can wrath long conflict
press.
Well may each soul feel all thy power to
bless,
Which the whole world is striving to attain. 10
Without thee lieth slain
Whatever power we have of doing good;
E'en as a picture in the darkness seen,
Which cannot so be showed,
Nor give delight of varied skill and scene. 15

CANZONE XII

1 The *Canzone* is quoted in *V. E.* ii. 5, 11. Winter has passed into spring, and with it come the sweet influences of love that warm men's blood Without love our best efforts are but as a picture in a dark place, where we can see neither form nor colour.

Upon my heart there smiteth still thy light,
As on the star, sun's ray,
Since that my soul as handmaid owned the sway,
From my first youth, of thy supernal power:
Hence a thought springs to life which guides her right, 20
With speech of subtle play,
To let my glance o'er each fair object stray
With more delight, the more it charms the hour.
And through this gazing, to my spirit's bower
A Maiden fair, who hath enslaved me, came, 25
And in me kindled flame,
As water, through its clearness, kindleth fire;
For at her coming those bright rays of thine,
With splendour I admire,
In those her fair eyes upward leap and shine. 30

Fair as she is in essence, and benign
In act, and full of love,
So still my fancy, which doth restless rove,
Doth paint her in my mind, where is her seat.
Not that it is itself so subtly fine 35
Such high emprise to prove,
But in thy might it onward dares to move

16 As the light to the eye, so is the light of love to the poet's heart. Therefore he turns to all forms of visible beauty, and so a maiden presents herself to him, in whom we recognise the familiar features of Philosophy as the "*donna gentile.*" Cold herself, she, like a glass sphere full of water, kindles fire. One notes the similitude as coming from the student of natural science (*Par.* ii 97-102). Possibly, however, the words may simply describe the reflection of fire in water.

17 Mediæval astronomy taught that the light of the fixed stars as well as of the planets was derived from the sun (*Par.* xxiii. 30, *n.*).

31 Yet it is not so much her own beauty in itself as the power of love that works through it that sways the soul. So fire neither

Beyond the power which Nature gives to us.
And with thy power her beauty groweth thus
As we may judge of work wrought out complete, 40
On subject fit and meet,
E'en as the sun is archetype of fire,
Which nor gives power to him nor takes away,
But lifts elsewhere far higher
The blissful influence of his glorious ray. 45

Therefore, O Sire, of such a nature kind,
That this nobility,
Bestowed on earth, and all benignity
Doth from thy fount on high for ever flow,
Look on my life, my life so hard, with mind 50
And look of sympathy;
For thy fierce heat, through her fair majesty,
Pervades my heart with great excess of woe.
Oh! by thy sweetness, Love, cause her to know
The great desire I have on her to look; 55
I pray thee do not brook
That she, in her fresh youth, my life should wrong;
For she as yet sees not how she doth please,
Nor how my love is strong,
Nor how that in her eyes she bears my peace. 60

adds to the sun's heat nor takes away, yet primarily derives its power from the sun as the source of all light and heat.

46 Therefore the poet prays love to help him to make the object of his love feel how greatly he desires to see her. Without that knowledge she, in her youthful beauty, might inflict a pain which she would shrink from inflicting, simply because she did not know that in her eyes her lover found his peace.

Great honour will be thine if thou shalt aid,
And mine a gift full rare,
Beyond all knowledge, for I now am there,
Where e'en my life I can no more defend;
For all my spirits are so spent and frayed, 65
That scarce can I declare,
Unless thy will shall pardon their despair,
How they can long endure, nor have an end.
Still to thy power shall men in homage bend,
In this fair Lady seen of worthiest might; 70
For still, it seems, 'tis right,
To give her of all good great company,
As one who in the world her station took
To hold her sovereignty
Over the minds of all that on her look. 75

Song, to the three least guilty of our land
Take thou thy way before thou elsewhere go;
Salute the two, and see thy power thou show,
To draw the third from evil company:
Tell them that good against good lifts not
hand, 80
Before with evil ones its strength it show:
Tell them that he is mad who doth not know,
Through fear of shame, from madness far to
flee.
He only fears who shrinks from war with ill,
For fleeing this all good he gains at will. 85

61 Such is the state in which the singer finds himself, that unless love comes to his aid, destruction seems imminent. Will he not incline the fair one to thoughts of pity?

76 The "envoy" of the *Canzone* is not admitted by Witte and Krafft as belonging to it. We ask in vain, in any case, who were the three least guilty to whom it was addressed. The names which suggest themselves as possible are Dino Compagni, G. Villani, Jacopo di Certaldo (*Fawr.* i. 201). Some light might be thrown on the politics of Florence and on Dante's life if we could discover why two out of the three are simply greeted, while the third

CANZONE XIII

LOVE'S SERVICE

Io sento sì d' Amor la gran possanza

I FEEL so much the potency of Love
  That I may not endure
Long while to suffer; whence I sorrow so,
Because his might doth hourly stronger prove,
  And I feel mine so poor 5
Become, from wonted use I fall below.
I ask not Love beyond my wish to go;
For should he do as much as will demands,
That strength which Nature gave into my
    hands
Would fail to meet it, vanquished in the strife: 10
And this is that which worketh keenest woe,
That power keeps not its faith to will's com-
    mands;
But if in will to good our guerdon stands,
I ask to gain a little longer life
From that sweet splendour of the beauteous
    eyes, 15
Which comfort brings, to soothe Love's agonies.

receives a special exhortation to amend his ways. If we could assume a date for the *Canzone* before A.D. 1300, we might think of Guido Cavalcanti as failing to sympathise with his friend's pursuit of Philosophy, and drifting to an epicurean materialism.

CANZONE XIII

[1] The consuming power of love brings pain and the sense of impotence. Strength must be sought from the bright eyes of the beloved one, *i.e.*, as in *Conv.* ii. 16, from the "demonstrations of Philosophy."

The rays of those bright eyes find entrance
wide
To mine, which Love doth sway
And where I bitter taste, they sweetness bear,
And know the road, as travellers who have
tried, 20
Before, the well-trod way;
And know the place where they with Love did
fare,
When through mine eyes they brought and
left him there.
Wherefore they turn to me and show me grace:
And they wrong her, whose service I embrace, 25
Hiding from me who love with such keen fire,
That only for her service life is dear;
And all my thoughts, where Love fills every space,
As to their banner, to her service pace:
Wherefore to work for her I so desire 30
That if I thought 'twould please her I should
fly,
Light were the task, yet know I, I should die.

Full true is Love which thus hath captured me
And bindeth me full fast,
Since I would do for him what now I say; 35
For no love with that love compared may be,
Which finds its joy at last
In death, another's wishes to obey:
And over me such purpose held its sway,

17 Those eyes have such a power to kindle love that the poet's life is only dear to him so far as it enables him to serve her. Yes, if it would please her, he would be content to leave her, though he knows that it would bring death.

33 The highest form of love is to seek death, if only that may be a true form of service and help to the beloved one. He is her servant, in the true sense of the word, a *cavaliere servente*. If her youth (possibly his own youth or his inexperience as a student of Philosophy) denies him a present reward, he is content to wait.

As soon as that strong passion, in its might, 40
Was born from the exceeding great delight
Of her fair face in whom all beauty dwells.
Her slave am I, and when my fond thoughts
stray
On what she is, I am contented quite.
For well against his will may man serve right; 45
And if my youth all hope of prize repels,
I wait a time when reason shall mature,
If only life may long enough endure.

When in my thoughts on longing sweet I
dwell,
Of greater longings born, 50
Which all my power to deeds of goodness
woo,
My payment seems my service to excel;
And with more wrong is borne
By me, so deem I, name of servant true;
Thus in her eyes in whom my joy I view, 55
Service is found, at others' hands, full pay.
But since beyond the truth I will not stray,
'Tis meet such longing should as service
count,
For if I seek my labours to pursue,
Not so on mine own good my fond thoughts
stay 60
As upon hers who o'er me holdeth sway.
For this I do that she may higher mount;
And I am wholly hers, attaining this,
That Love has made me worthy of such bliss.

[49] Nay, but he is more than paid for a service which is its own exceeding great reward. His service too is little more than the will to serve, but the will may be counted for the deed.

No power but Love could me of such mood make,[65]
  That I might worthily
Belong to her who yields not to Love's sway,
But stands as queen, who little heed doth take
  Of love's intensity,
Who without her can never pass a day. 70
Ne'er have I seen her but she did display
A beauty new that still in her I found,
Whence in me Love's great might doth more
      abound,
E'en as new joy is added to the old;
And hence it chances that I still do stay 75
In one condition, and Love me doth meet
With such keen anguish and such rapture sweet,
For all the time he lays on me his hold,
Which lasts from when I lost her from my view,
E'en to that hour when she is seen anew. 80

My Canzon' fair, if thou art like to me,
  Thou wilt not look with scorn
As much as might befit thy goodness sweet;
Wherefore I pray that thou learn subtlety,
  Dear song of true Love born, 85
To take the way and method that is meet.
If true knight thee with offered welcome greet;

[65] Yet his passion is not returned. She (Philosophy) looks calmly on. While he finds fresh beauty in her face, a new pain and a new joy, he does not find in her the fruition which he seeks. She does not satisfy his quenchless thirst (*Conv.* iii. 15, iv. 12, 13). In *Par.* iii. 70–90 we have the report of a different and higher experience.

[81] As with *Canz.* xii., so here the "*envoi*" seems to conceal a hidden meaning. Is this "sect," the members of which alone it is to trust, that of the seekers after wisdom, or Ghibelline idealists? Each theory has its supporters. So the wicked of the last line are either generally those who sin against truth and righteousness, or especially the Guelph Neri of Florence. This stanza, it may be noted, is not found in many MSS., and some editors (Witte) have put the last stanza of *Canz.* xii. in the place which Fraticelli assigns to this.

Before thou yield thyself to do his will,
See if his soul with thy love thou canst fill,
And if thou canst not, quickly let him go; 90
For good with good still sitteth on one seat,
But oft it chances one doth find him still
In such a company he fares but ill,
Through evil fame that others on him blow.
With the base dwell not, or in mind or heart; 95
For never was it wise to take their part.

CANZONE XIV

THE ANGELS OF THE THIRD HEAVEN

Voi, che, intendendo, il terzo ciel movete

Ye who with wisdom high the third heaven move,
Hear ye the reasonings that are in my heart;
I may not others tell, they seem so new.
The sphere whose motion from your might doth start,

CANZONE XIV

This *Canzone* has for us the interest of being the first of the fourteen of which the *Convito*, had it been completed, would have been the exposition, and which is accordingly expounded at length in *Conv.* ii. In that work he defends himself against the charge of having transferred the love which he had given to Beatrice to another human object, and explains that the lady of whom the *Canzone* speaks is none other than Philosophy, the daughter of the great Emperor of the Universe. I agree with Witte and Krafft in looking on the allegorical explanation as an afterthought, and hold that the "letter" of a true history is to be found. *V. N.* c. 36-40.

1 The third heaven is the sphere of Venus, as in *Par.* viii. 1-12; *Conv.* ii. 6. And in accordance with Dante's astronomy it is

Kind beings that ye are and full of love, 5
Me to this state in which I now live drew;
Whence of the life I lead, an utterance true
To you might be addressed most worthily.
Wherefore I pray you that ye give me ear:
I of my heart to you new tidings bear 10
How my sad soul breathes there full many a
sigh,
And how a spirit pleads those sighs to bar,
Which cometh in the rays of your bright star.

As life in my sad heart was wont to be
A tender thought which oftentimes would
go, 15
And of your Lord and Master seek the feet,
Where a fair dame it saw all glorious show,
Of whom it spoke to me so pleasantly,
That my soul said, "I too would thither
fleet."
Now appears one who bids that thought
retreat; 20
And with such great might lords it over me,
That my heart throbs and brings its grief to
light.
He on another lady turns my sight,
And saith, "Who seeks true blessedness to
see,
Let him upon the eyes of this dame look, 25
If he can sighs and anguish bravely brook."

moved by angels, or, more scientifically, by intelligent powers (*Conv.* iv. 19), whose volition suffices for that purpose (*Par.* viii. 37, xxvii. 114). The influence of that planet has made him sorrowful. He will tell them the tale of his woe. A comparison of *V. N.* c. 36 with *Conv.* ii. 2, 13, fixes the date of the *Canzone* between 1292 and 1295, probably in the latter year.

14 The sweet thought is the memory of Beatrice as now glorified. He would fain draw near to her. But then another thought drives that out. There is a new master-passion. The love of Philosophy

A spirit findeth, hostile to the death,
That meek thought that was wont to speak to me
Of a dear angel, who is crowned in Heaven.
My soul bewails, so great its misery, 30
And saith, "Alas! how from me vanisheth
That piteous thought which me hath comfort given,"
Speaks of mine eyes, and saith this soul grief-riven,
"What hour was that such lady them beheld?
And why believed they not my speech of her?" 35
I said, "Needs must he have his station there
In her bright eyes, who all my peers hath quelled;"
And it availed not when I her had seen
That they saw him not, who my death hath been.

"Thou art not dead, but thou art stupefied, 40
O soul of mine, who dost so sadly wail."
So speaks a spirit filled with gentlest love,
"For this fair dame who o'er thee doth prevail,
Hath all thy life so changed and modified,

(I use the term to distinguish it from the heavenly wisdom of which Beatrice was the representative) is driving out the memory of the past.

27 Still, however, that memory, as of an angel crowned in heaven, keeps its ground. But then, so far as it does, the new consoling passion withdraws its influence and its joy. So he is in a strait between two. Was it not an evil day when Philosophy drew him from Beatrice? He knows that that new passion slays the peace of those who have resumed the common pleasures and low ambitions of mankind (*Conv.* ii. 16), or who, like himself, are eager to plunge into all mysteries and all knowledge.

40 The spirit of Love pleads the cause of Philosophy. It was not death, but fear that oppressed him. The new mistress of his

That thou fear'st her, so recreant dost thou
 prove; 45
Behold how meek and gracious she doth
 move,
How courteous in her greatness, and how
 wise;
And in thy thought thy mistress let her be,
For if thyself thou do not cheat, thou'lt see
Such wealth of marvels and of mysteries, 50
That thou wilt say, 'O Love, mine own true
 Lord,
Behold thine handmaid; work thou out thy
 word.'"

Canzon', I deem that they will be but few
Who will thy meaning rightly understand,
So difficult and laboured is thy speech: 55
Whence if, perchance, such fortune thee
 attend
That thou thy way to any should'st pursue
Who seem not 'ware what lore thine accents
 teach,
I pray thee then, thou yet some comfort
 reach,
By telling them, my tender, darling lamb, 60
"At least take heed how beautiful I am."

soul had transformed his life, and, if he were faithful to her, he would see yet greater wonders. Then his soul would be able to say, "Behold thy handmaid; work thou thy will on me" (*Purg*. x. 44). The words are quoted in the last-named passage, however, as an example of the humility which in the later stage of his spiritual life the poet had found to be more precious even than Philosophy. Here again the *Commedia* is the recantation of the *Convito*.

53 There is obviously a sense of satisfaction in the thought that the *Canzone* will be "caviare to the general." The poet's desire is to speak what the wise will understand, while even those who fail to grasp the inner meaning cannot fail to admire the beauty of the verse. The *tornata* is translated in the *Preface* to Shelley's *Epipsychidion*.

CANZONE XV

THE MIRACLE OF BEAUTY

Amor che nella mente mi ragiona

LOVE, who doth often with my mind converse,
In eager longing, of my Lady fair,
Often of her doth utter things so rare
That all my reason goes thereon astray.
His speech such strains of sweetness doth
rehearse, 5
That my weak soul that listens and doth
hear,
Doth say, "Ah me! for I no power do bear
To tell what he doth of my Lady say.
'Tis certain it behoves I put away,
If I would treat of what I hear of her, 10
That which my mind fails utterly to reach,
And much of clearer speech;
For want of knowledge then would me
deter."

Wherefore if these my rhymes be found to fail,
Which fain a worthy praise would minister, 15
My feeble mind let all the blame assail,
And this our speech which hath no power to
spell
All that of her it hears Love often tell.

CANZONE XV

1-18 The second of the poems expounded in the *Convito* (B. iii.). As in *Purg.* xxiv. 52, the poet claims the merit of writing as love taught him to write. But he feels the impotence of speech to repro-

The Sun, that all the world encompasseth,
Sees nothing half so lovely any hour, 20
As when he shines where resteth in her bower
The Lady for whose praise my tongue Love frees.
Each spirit high sees her and wondereth,
And all the tribe that here own Love's sweet power,
Shall find her presence as their thoughts' high dower, 25
When Love gives them perception of her peace;
So doth her nature Him who gives it please,
Who aye in her His virtue doth infuse
Beyond our Nature's utmost claim or plea.
The soul of purity, 30
Which this great grace of healing power imbues,
That gift displays, in that which it doth guide,
For her fair form is that which eyesight views;
And still their eyes who in her light abide
Send envoys to the heart whose wishes rise 35
In the clear air, and take the form of sighs.

duce what he has thus heard of his beloved one, the Philosophy who now sways his soul. For a time, on which he afterwards looked back with self-reproach and penitence (*Purg.* xxxi. 55-60), the conflict described in *Canz.* xiv. had ceased, and Beatrice was practically superseded and dethroned by the new passion.

19-36 The parable is so well sustained, that, but for the exposition in *Conv.* iii., we should be half tempted to think that it was Beatrice, and not Philosophy that is spoken of. We have, as in *Prov.* viii. 22-31, *Wisd.* vii. 22-30, a picture of the beauty of Wisdom clad in visible form, whose eyes are the higher and more transcendent truths which she reveals to those who seek her. It is noticeable that the sapiential books of the Bible—Proverbs, Ecclesiastes, Wisdom, Ecclesiasticus—are those which he chiefly quotes in the

On her God's grace descendeth from on high,
As on an angel who His presence sees,
And if a gentle Lady's faith should cease,
Walk she with her, and see her bearing sweet. 40
There, where she speaks, doth ever downward fly,
A heavenly spirit witnessing with these
How the high power she owns by heaven's decrees
Goes beyond all things that for us are meet.
The gentle acts wherewith she all doth greet 45
Go calling upon Love in rivalry,
With speech that makes him lend a listening ear.
Of her we this may hear.
"What in fair dame is kind in her we see,
And she is fair who most resembles her." 50
And we may hear that this her beauty free
Helps to gain faith for what doth wonder stir,
And thus our faith doth confirmation gain
From her, for this the Eternal did ordain.

Things in her aspect are made manifest 55
That witness of the bliss of Paradise;
Of her sweet smile I speak, and beaming eyes,
Which Love brings there, the place of their desire.
Our feeble mind by them is all opprest,

Convito. Then he thought that they spoke of the purely intellectual philosophy to which he had devoted himself. Afterwards he learnt to connect them with the higher spiritual wisdom of which not the "*donna gentile*," but Beatrice was the symbol.

37-54 In that Philosophy there is a virtue like that which belongs to the angel who stands in the presence of God, as the Cherubim and Seraphim stand (*Par.* xxi. 92). Whatever there is of gentleness and beauty in human form is but the reflection of her loveliness.

55-72 In her beauty, her eyes, and her smile there is the joy of

As when the sun on vision weak doth rise: 60
And since I may not gaze in steadfast wise,
Needs must I not beyond short speech aspire.
Her beauty showers down tongues of living fire,
All animate with spirit good and kind,
Which is the parent of all noble thought; 65
And as with lightning fraught
They break the innate sins which shame and blind.
Wherefore if any lady thinks that less
Of praise she hath for looks of haughty mind,
Let her behold this type of lowliness. 70
She is it who doth humble hearts perverse;
She was His thought, who launched the universe.

My Song, it seems thou speak'st in diverse tones
From speech that came from sister fair of thine;
For this fair lady, who with thee doth shine 75
As lowly, she calls proud and arrogant.
Thou know'st that heaven is clear and bright alone,
And in itself nought mars its light divine,
But for full many a cause these eyes of mine

Paradise. The vices that cloud the soul perish in her presence. And yet she is the pattern of all lowliness, even while she brings low the perverseness of the proud. The eyes and the smile remind us of Beatrice in *Par.* xxi. 1, xxii. 11, xxiii. 48, but the comparison of the two descriptions leads to the conclusion that what is here said of Philosophy is re-transferred afterwards, in the closing and higher experience, to the diviner Wisdom.

73-90 The reference is to *Ball.* x., in which he had spoken of the mistress of his soul, now identified with Philosophy, as proud and disdainful, as in *Canz.* vi. Dante looks on his poems as forming a sisterhood of song. The explanation of the apparent contradiction is that the eye sees what it has the power to see. The sun, or, better perhaps, the starry firmament, seems dim to those whose sight is weak (a touch, it may be, of personal experience, *Conv.* iii. 9), and Wisdom seems stern to those who are yet in the early stages of their search after her. The reader will remember the two faces

Deem the sun's glory dimmed as by a cloud. 80
Thus, when thy sister calls her stern and
proud,
She thinks not of her as she is in truth,
But only as to her she doth appear;
For my soul lived in fear,
And feareth still, so that devoid of ruth 85
She seems, when I perceive she seeth me.
Thus plead, if any need arise, in sooth,
And when thou com'st, and she shall look
on thee,
Say thou, "O Lady, if it please thee well,
I will on every side thy praises tell." 90

CANZONE XVI

TRUE NOBILITY

Le dolci rime d' amore, ch' io solia

THE pleasant rhymes of Love which 'twas my
care
To seek out in my mind,
I now must leave, not that no hope I find
To turn to them again;
But that the mien disdainful and unkind, 5
Which in my lady fair

of Wisdom in Giotto's fresco at Assisi. Comp. also *Ecclus.* iv. 17, 18, and *Ball.* x., *n.*

CANZONE XVI

1-20 The third of the *Convito* poems, expounded in *B.* iv. The thought of the reserved and, as it were, disdainful aspect of Wisdom,

Hath shown itself, hath barred the thorough-
fare
Of wonted speech and plain.
And since to wait good reason doth con-
strain,
I now will lay aside my sweeter style, 10
Which, when I write of love, pervadeth all,
And that high worth recall,
Through which a man grows noble without
guile,
With keen sharp rhymes awhile
Reproving still the judgment false and vile 15
Of those who think that true nobility
In hoarded wealth doth lie;
And, at the outset on that Lord I call,
Who makes his dwelling in my Lady's eyes,
Whereby in her love of herself doth rise. 20

One ruled of old, who thought nobility—
So he, at least, did deem—
In ancient wealth was found and high
esteem
With ordered life and fair:
Another did of poorer wisdom seem, 25
Who scorned that maxim high,

to which reference had been made in the last stanza of *Canz.* xv., returns, and therefore the poet will for a time cease to sing her praises and turn to another subject, the nature of true nobility. He wishes to show how false is the judgment of the crowds who identify it with wealth. One may trace, if I mistake not, in this change of subject the beginning of the dissatisfaction with the pursuit of Philosophy which uttered itself in the confessions of *Purg.* xxxi and the joy of the *Paradiso*. He had found himself face to face with problems which he could not solve, and which he afterwards came to look upon as trivial (*Conv.* iv. 2; *Par.* xiii. 97–102).

21-40 The saying discussed is traditionally referred (we have nothing, however, but the tradition) to the Emperor Frederick II. That saying was but partially true at the best. Others had brought it down to a yet lower level by omitting the condition expressed in its closing words. Ancestry and wealth were believed to be an adequate definition of nobility.

And thereof let the latter clause go by,
Having, perchance, nought there.
And after such as he all others fare,
Who reckon noble men by ancestry, 30
Which for long years hath run through wealthy line.
And so long such malign,
False judgment among us hath come to be,
That him distinguish we
As noble who can say, "Behold in me 35
Grandson or son of knight who nobly fought,"
Though his own worth be nought:
But basest he to those who truth divine,
Who sees the road and then doth turn aside,
Like one who, dead, doth yet on earth abide. 40

Whoso defined man as "a tree that lives"
First says what is not true,
And with that falsehood takes defective view;
May be, he sees no more.
So he who weighty cares of empire knew, 45
False definition gives;
For first he speaks what's false, and next perceives
But half the truer lore.
For neither, as men think, can wealth's full store,

41-60 The definition is as imperfect as though one should define man as a living tree, which would only be so far true as it predicated life as part of man's being. Riches, as such, can give no real nobleness of character. The comparison that follows indicates Dante's insight into the secret of all completeness in art. The artist who paints must become like that which he depicts, or else he fails. "Fra Angelico could not paint the fiery glow of passion, nor

Or give nobility, or take away, 50
Because of its own nature it is base.
For he who paints a face
Must first *be* that, ere picture it he may:
Nor can the river sway
A steadfast tower, as it from far doth stray. 55
That wealth is vile and incomplete 'tis
plain;
However much we gain,
It brings no rest, but heaps up cares apace;
Wherefore the soul that upright is and true,
Their loss with calm and tranquil mind doth
view. 60

Nor let men deem a base churl can attain
To honour true; or that from churlish sire
A race may spring that shall to fame aspire:
This by them stands confest;
Thus do their self-confuted proofs retire, 65
So far as they maintain
That time to honour true doth appertain,
As is by them exprest.
And hence it follows from what they attest
That all of us or noble are or base, 70
Or that man never had beginning true:
But I take not this view,

Michael Angelo the joy of devout resignation" (*Witte*). The other simile compares true nobility to the tower standing on a rock, past which the stream of earthly fortune and its chances flow by, leaving it unshaken. Comp. *H.* vii. 61-96.

71-80 The other part of the definition is now discussed. Does nobility depend on a long line of ancestors? To assert this is to run counter to facts. The common man may rise; the high-born man may fall. Yes; there must have been a time in every family when its founder first rose to greatness, and became noble though he had no noble ancestors. If the noble and the vulgar are so only by heredity, then we are all of us gentle or simple by birth; but that assumption is at variance with the doctrine of the unity of the human race as descended from Adam, and therefore no Christian

Nor even they, if they have Christian grace.
To minds in healthy case,
'Tis therefore clear their maxims have no base, 75
And therefore them as false I still reprove,
And far from them remove,
And now will, as I think, proclaim anew,
What is the true Noblesse, and whence it springs,
And what the notes that name of 'noble' brings. 80

I say each virtue, in inception,
Comes from a single root,
Virtue, I mean, with happiness as fruit,
In all its actions right;
This is—so with our Ethics following suit— 85
Right choice to habit grown,
The which doth dwell in the true mean alone,
And such words brings to light.
I say that Noblesse doth, by reason's might,
Connote all good in him of whom 'tis said; 90
As baseness evermore connoteth ill:
And such a virtue still

can receive it. Dante had learnt that lesson from his favourite, Boethius (iii. 6):—

"*Omne hominum genus in terris*
Simili surgit ab ortu,
Unus enim pater est
Unus qui cuncta ministrat."

The two false definitions being cleared away, the ground is open for a truer definition.

81-100 That definition is found in the thought that wherever there is virtue there we recognise nobility. It does not follow, however, that the definition is convertible. There may be a nobility of character, as in youth or maiden, in whom virtue is not yet ethically complete, whose modest shyness is, in fact, not a virtue, but almost a defect. Let no man, therefore, boast that he is noble

Gives knowledge of itself to those that seek;
Since 'neath the self-same head
Both meet, in one effect accomplishèd; 95
Whence needs must be that this from that should spring,
Or each some third cause bring;
But if this with the other like worth fill,
And more, that other rather springs from this:
Proceed we then on this hypothesis. 100

Noblesse wherever virtue dwells is found,
Virtue where noblesse, no;
E'en as 'tis heaven where'er the sun doth go,
Though not so the converse;
And we see ladies in their youth's fresh glow, 105
With this great blessing crowned,
So far as they in shamefastness abound,
From virtue yet diverse.
Hence must proceed, as from black cometh perse,
From this last every virtue singular, 110
Or from the parent-stock of all the host.
Wherefore let no man boast,
Saying, "By descent her fellowship I share,"
For all but gods they are
Who have such grace with every fault afar. 115

because he has a long pedigree. God alone gives the true nobility, and those who have it are sharers, so to speak, in the Divine nature.

101-120 The beauty of the *Canzone* rises to its highest point, and we have an ideal picture of a noble life in all its successive stages, the obedience and modesty of childhood, the temperance and manliness of youth, the wisdom, justice, munificence of maturity, the contemplative devotion of old age. In the last we trace an echo of what he had learnt from Cic. *de Senectute*. The thought of the re-wedding of the soul to God meets us in *Purg.* xxiii. 81.

For God alone bestows it on the mind,
Which He doth perfect find,
Resting in Him; so that in few at most
The seed of perfect blessedness is sown,
Planted by God in souls to fitness grown. 120

The soul whom that high goodness doth adorn,
Doth not its presence hide,
For from the first she, as the body's bride,
Herself till death displays.
Obedient, gentle, modest, far from pride, 125
Is she in life's young morn;
And decks herself with many a grace new-born,
In Wisdom's perfect ways;
Constant and temperate in life's young days,

141-146 The "*envoi*" bids the *Canzone* speed to the mistress of the poet's soul, *i.e.*, to Philosophy. She will recognise its truth.

We are so familiar with the sentiments embodied in this poem, that they come to us almost as commonplace platitudes. We must put ourselves into the poet's position, as standing apart, on the one side, from the old feudal nobility of Florence, as represented by the Uberti, Rusticucci, and others, and, on the other, from the *nouveaux riches*, represented by the Bardi, the Cerchi, and the Frescobaldi, to understand how he may have seemed to himself to be uttering a new or neglected truth with almost prophetic solemnity. In reaching that truth he had to renounce not only the dominant falsehood of his time, but even the authority of his great master, Aristotle (*Pol.* iii. 12, 13), who assigns to ancestral wealth (ἀρχαιόπλουτοι) a far larger share in nobility than Dante does, and to fall back upon what we have learnt to call the "flesh and blood" argument of the brotherhood of mankind, as children of the same earthly and the same heavenly Father. If there was any special nobleness in any man that raised him above his fellows, it was the gift of God. In *Conv.* iv. 20 he refers to his master, Guido Guinicelli, as teaching the same truth in the Sonnet, "*Al cor gentile ripara sempre amore.*" In doing so he follows Aquinas (*Summ.* ii. 2. 134, 3), where he ceased to follow Aristotle (*Ozan.* pp. 397-398). Comp. also Ægidius Columna (*De Regim. Principum*, iii. 2, 8). Two of his favourite poets, Ovid and Juvenal, were probably among his teachers in this matter, and we can

Full of sweet love and praiseful courtesy, 130
And finds in loyal deeds her sole delight;
In age's gathering night,
Prudent and just and of her bounty free;
And in her soul joys she
To hear or tell how worthy others be. 135
And then she reaches life's fourth period
Re-married unto God,
Waiting her end in contemplation's light,
And blesseth all the seasons of the past.
See now how many have in lies been cast! 140

Thou, 'gainst those erring ones, my Song,
shalt speed,
And when thou art, indeed,

scarcely fail to recognise echoes of their words in Dante's teaching. Thus Ovid (*Met.* xiii. 140)—

"*At genus, et proavos, et quæ non fecimus ipsi,*
Vix ea nostra voco."

Or Juvenal, *Sat.* viii. 272-276—

"*Et tamen, ut longe repetas longeque revolvas,*
Nomen, ab infami gentem deducis asylo.
Majorum primus quisquis fuit ille tuorum
Aut pastor fuit, aut illud quod dicere nolo."

Or again Juvenal, *Sat.* viii. 20 –

"*Tota licet veteres exornent undique ceræ*
Atria, nobilitas sola est atque unica virtus."

In connection with Dante's other writings and with his life, we may note (1) that he has risen to a higher level of thought than that of which we find traces in *H.* xv. 77; (2) that many of his examples of goodness and greatness seem specially chosen to illustrate the ideal for which he is here contending, as, *e.g.*, Romeo in *Par.* vi. 128-142, Pier Pettinagno in *Purg.* xiii. 128; (3) that he speaks in the same tone, as of one who had conquered an error under the power of which he had himself at one time lived, in *Purg.* xiii. 133-138; *Par.* xvi. 1-9. We may also, I think, reasonably conjecture that the *Canzone* was written when he was looking for the appearance of Henry VII. as the restorer of an ideal empire, by the virtues the absence of which had made Frederick II. its destroyer, and that it had a direct political purpose in itself, and yet more as expounded in *Conv.* iv., as setting before that Emperor the principles on which he was to act. If, with Fraticelli in *O. M.* iii. 31-33, we infer from *Conv.* iv. 3, 6, 16,

There where our lady fair her home doth find,
Let not thine errand from her hidden be;
Tell her in verity, 145
"I of thy true friend come to speak my mind."

that the *Canzone* was written before 1300—and I must own that his arguments are of considerable weight—then we must look on the manifesto as addressed to an ideal ruler such as he contemplated when he wrote the *De Monarchiâ* or *H.* i. 101-104. Lastly, it is interesting to note the fact that few if any of Dante's minor poems have so impressed themselves on the minds of the generation that followed. Comp. *e.g.*, Cecco d' Ascoli (*L' Acerba*, ii. 12, quoted in Frat. *O. M.*, i. p. 190), and our own Chaucer, who quotes from it as follows:—

"Here may ye see well how that genterie
Is not annexed to possession,
. . . . .
For God it wot, men may ful often find
A lordes son do shame and vilanie.
And he that would have prise of genterie
For he was boren of a gentil hous,
And had his elders noble and vertuous,
And n' ill himself do no gentil dedes,
Ne folowe his gentil auncester that ded is,
He n' is not gentil, be he duk or erl;
For vilain's sinful dedes make a cherl;
For gentilesse n' is but the renomee
Of thine auncestres, for hir high bountie,
Which is a strange thing to thy persone;
Thy gentilesse cometh from God alone."
—*Wife of Bath's Tale.*

CANZONE XVII

VIRTUS SOLA NOBILITAS

Poscia ch' Amor del tutto m'ha lasciato

SINCE Love hath ceased my longing soul to fill,
Not by my choice of will,
For still a gladder state I could not know,
But that he pitied so
That anguish of my heart— 5
To listen to my wail he could not bear.
Thus, disenamoured, I my song will trill
Against that form of ill
Which will its speech in terms perverse
bestow,
And call the base and low 10
By name of worthiest part,

CANZONE XVII

1-19 In its form this *Canzone* presents a singular complication. Each stanza of nineteen lines is divided into four sub-stanzas, the first of four lines, the other three of five lines each. In each of the first two, after two terminal rhymes at the beginning of the sub-stanza, the rhyme is repeated, as in the translation, in the middle of the third line. In the *V. E.* (ii. 12) Dante refers to this *Canzone*, obviously with a special satisfaction, as giving the effect in this peculiar rhyming of what he calls an "answering echo." In its matter it is a kind of corollary from *Cans.* xvi. Men have false notions on other matters besides nobility. They call evil good and good evil, and give the name of gallantry, which ought to include virtue aud liberality, to its counterfeits. We are reminded of Tennyson's protest against those who thus abuse the "grand old name of gentleman."

1-3 The lines find a parallel in the old Latin hymn—

"*Blandus hic dolor est,*
Qui meus amor est;"

and in the lines of Guido of Arezzo (*Cans.* xxxvi.)—

"*Tutto 'l dolor ch' io mai portai fu gioja.*"—(*Witte.*

The name of "gallantry," which sounds so
fair,
That worthy of the rare
Imperial robe it makes him whom it sways.
This the true flag displays 15
Which indicates where Virtue hath her home,
Whence I am sure if her my speech defend
E'en as I apprehend,
That once more Love with favouring grace
shall come.

There are who, squandering all their wealth
away, 20
Believe that thus they may
Their way make thither where the good abide,
Who after death provide
A home within the mind
Of whosoever owneth wisdom true; 25
But to please good men this is not the way;
For greed as wisdom they
Display, and thus would 'scape full many an
ill,
To th' error cleaving still,
Of them and of their kind, 30
In whom false teaching doth their lore
imbue.
Who will not folly view
In banquets rich and light luxurious play,
And proud and rich array,

20-38 So men looked on prodigality as a sign of generosity. Dante, as in *H.* vii. 25-30, and in the teaching of Statius (*Purg.* xxii. 31-45), saw that extremes meet, and that it stood on the same footing of guilt as the avarice which was apparently its opposite (*Conv.* iv. 27). What good was there in spending money in banquets or dress. Manners, not clothes, make the man. Line 35 seems to point to the Italian practice of decorating animals that

As if for sale where buyers are unwise? 35
Not by his dress the wise a man's worth
know—
This is but outward show—
But praise true wisdom and brave courtesies.

Others there are who, by the ready sneer,
Would fain appear, 40
Wit-clear, and prompt in ready intellect,
To hearers who are tricked
As they behold them smile
At what their mind doth fail to understand.
They speak in words that show of wisdom
wear, 45
And count it dear,
To hear themselves with vulgar praises
decked.
Love ne'er did them affect
With ladies' love awhile:
In converse they all base jests have at
hand, 50
Ne'er would their foot have spanned
One pace for lady's sake, in knightly wise:
But as to robberies
The thief, haste they to steal some pleasure
base;
But not in ladies yet doth fade and die 5
True sense of gallantry,
That they should seem to lose all wisdom's
trace.

are exposed for sale in a public market, as *e.g.*, in the Campo Vaccino at Rome.

39-57 So, too, men passed for wise because they could smile superciliously. That might win the praise of the vulgar, but they know not what true praise or true love is. Their speech is cynical, their pleasures base. To the women who are worthy of love they are little better than beasts that have no understanding.

Virtue that leaves the straight path is not pure,
And hence of blame is sure;
Endure she cannot when we virtue need, 60
In those the good in deed,
By the true Spirit led,
Or habit which on Wisdom lays fast hold.
Therefore, if praise of it in knight endure,
Its cause we find in ure, 65
Full sure, of many mixed things; since indeed
It doth with one succeed,
With others falleth dead.
But Virtue pure its place in all doth hold.
Delight, that doth enfold 70
Within it love, hath thus the work perfected.
And by this last directed
Is gallantry, and hath her being there,
E'en as the sun, which gathers in its might
Round it both warmth and light, 75
Together with its form of beauty fair.

Though star with star should, with commingled ray,
Turn gallantry away
To stray, as much and more than I may tell,
Yet I, who know it well, 80
Thanks to a gentle one,
Who showed them to me in each action fair,

58-76 Virtue that leaves the true path is not pure. What is needed for its perfection, either as in the devout life or as in that of the students of wisdom, is the union of rectitude, and love, and pleasantness.

77-96 Though the aspect of the heavens is against true gallantry, yet the poet, who has seen it embodied in one he loved (obviously a reference to Beatrice), will not hold his peace. He knows not whom his song will reach. His hearers may be but few, but he must bear his witness that there is no true praise but that which is won by virtue. Witte inverts the order of the fourth and fifth tanzas.

Will not be silent, for I should display
 Base soul of mire and clay,
Alway, and with her enemies seem one. 85
 So I from this time on
 Will with song subtly rare,
Thereof speak truth, not knowing who will
  heed;
 But this I swear indeed,
By him whose name is Love, of bliss com-
  pact, 90
 That virtue without act
Can ne'er acquire the guerdon of true praise,
Therefore if this hold good in argument,
 As all will give assent,
'Twere virtue, and with virtue knit always. 95

To the great planet it is like, whose might,
 From sunrise bright
Till night when it conceals its glorious ray,
 And where its bright beams play,
 Pours life and strength below, 100
As that on which it shines may bear its
  power;
So she, in scorn of each unworthy wight
 Who, in false light,
True knight appears in form that so
  deceives,
 That fruits belie their leaves, 105
 Since ill deeds from them flow,
Like gifts upon the gentle heart doth
  shower;
 Quickly with life doth dower,

96-114 True virtue is like the sun (reckoned in mediæval astronomy among the planets), shedding light and heat all around (*Par.* xxii. 116). She scorns all counterfeits of good, and all unworthy knights are enemies of her who is as the sun in its glory.

With solace fair, and lovely manners new,
  Which each hour brings to view; 110
He who takes her takes virtue as his guide.
O ye false knights, perverse and craven ye,
  With her at enmity,
Who like the stars' king shineth far and
    wide.

He freely takes and gives whom she doth
    own, 115
  Nor is with grief o'erdone;
The sun grieves not when it to stars gives
    light,
  Nor when from them aright
  Comes help for its employ,
But each therein finds ever bliss renewed. 120
To wrath he never is by words urged on;
  But those alone,
Are known by him, that are both good and
    right,
  And all his speech is bright.
Dear for himself is he and full of joy, 125
  Desired by wise and good;
  For of the viler brood
He prizes equally the praise and blame;
  Nor, through the loftiest fame,

115-133 The giving and receiving of l. 115 are concerned not with money, but with knowledge. Dante may have had in his thoughts Augustine's application of the words "God loveth a cheerful giver" (*De Catech. Rud.* c. 14). Comp. *Conv.* i. 9. He in whom virtue dwells gives as the sun gives to the planets and the fixed stars, both of which were thought to derive from him their light, and grieves not, but rejoices in all reciprocity of good. He is not easily led to wrath, is dear to the wise, cares little for the praise or blame of the unwise, is not easily puffed up, shows his goodness to those who are worthy of it (*H.* ii. 61; *Purg.* xi. 100-120). Witte finds a parallel in the counsel given by St. Philip Neri, "*Spernere te sperni.*" Alas! the men that are now do just the opposite of all this.

Swells high with pride, but when the time
arrives 120
When it is fit that he his courage show,
There praise for him doth flow:
Far otherwise than this are most men's lives.

CANZONE XVIII

FREEDOM AND BONDAGE

Doglia mi reca nello core ardire

GRIEF brings within my heart a spirit bold
To help the will which loveth all that's true;
So, Ladies, if to you
I speak what seems against mankind as
thrown,
Marvel thereat the less; 5
But learn your low desires full cheap to
hold:
For beauty, which through love in you hath
grown
For virtue true alone,

CANZONE XVIII

1-21 The preacher now takes beauty as his text, and moralises much as he had done on gallantry. He may seem to say a strange thing, but if beauty is given to woman, and valour to man, that love may make of the twain one, then it were well that women should hide their beauty and turn away from love, for true virtue, as things are, is rarely to be found. Dante refers to this *Canzone* in the *V. E.* ii. 2 as an example of his work as the "poet of righteousness," and apparently (*Conv.* i. 8) it was intended to have been the groundwork of *Conv.* xv. had the poet completed that work. It is largely based upon Seneca, *De Beneficiis*, ii. 2.

By his decree of old was fashionèd;
Against which ye transgress. 10
I say to you who Love's great power confess,
That if your dower be beauty,
As ours is virtuous duty,
And unto him is given to make both one,
Ye ought all love to shun, 15
And cover what of beauty is your share,
For that it hath not virtue, love's true sign.
Ah, where drifts speech of mine?
Fair scorn do I opine,
Were rightly honoured in a lady fair, 20
Who should her beauty banish from her care.

Man from himself hath virtue driven away,
True man no more, but brute in man's estate:
Ah, God! what wonder great,
That man should wish from lord to slave to fall, 25
From life to death descend!
Virtue, to her Creator subject aye,
Obeys Him, giving Him true praise in all,
Ladies, that Love may call
Her as enrolled, where his true subjects wend, 30
In His blest court on high.
From the fair gates she cometh cheerfully,
And to her mistress turns,
Goes gladly and sojourns,

22-42 Yes; man has become brute (*Conv.* ii. 7), the master has become the slave. Virtue is ever true to her Creator, ready for any service, caring not for death, a possession that is a perpetual joy.

And with great joy fulfils her vassalage. 35
Through her short pilgrimage
She keeps, adorns, enriches what she finds,
And warreth so with death, he brings no fear:
O Maiden pure and dear,
Shaped in the heavenly sphere, 40
Thou only makest noble; proof is this
That thou the treasure art that bringeth bliss.

Slave, not of true lord, but of slave most base,
He makes himself who from this Master strays.
Hear now how dear he pays, 45
If ye count up his loss on either side,
Who passeth virtue by:
This master-slave works out such foul disgrace,
That the clear eyes that mental light provide
Through him their vision hide, 50
So that he needs must tread in others' ways,
Where madness meets his eye.
But that my words with profit may apply,
From whole I pass to part,
And to constructive art 55
More simple, that they tell an easier tale;
For seldom 'neath a veil
Doth speech obscure approach the mind aright,

43-63 Look on that picture and then on this. To serve Mammon is to be a "*servo signor*," the slave of a slave, and to find him the hardest of all taskmasters. That he may rescue men from such a bondage the poet will descend to particulars and use all plainness of speech.

And hence with you my wish is to speak plain.
This do I for your gain— 60
Not mine, I must explain—
That ye may hold each churl in deep despite;
For too soon likeness springeth from delight.

He who is slave is like a man who goes
In his lord's track, and knows not where it leads, 65
But in dark path proceeds;
So fares the miser seeking money still,
Which over all doth reign:
Swift runs the miser, swifter flies repose
(O blinded soul, that neither can nor will 70
Discern its wishes ill!)
With that heaped hoard which every hour exceeds,
And doth no goal attain.
Lo, they reach him who levelling doth reign:
Tell me, what hast thou won, 75
Blind miser, all undone?
Answer, if other answer be than nought.
With curse thy couch is fraught,

64-84 He who seeks to satisfy himself with riches attempts that which is impossible. He is trying to grasp the infinite, for "*Crescit amor nummi quantum ipsa pecunia crescit*," *Juv.* xiv. 139 (*Conv.* iii. 15). And when Death, the great leveller, comes, what does he find then? He can take nothing of all his heaped-up treasures into the region behind the veil. We are reminded of the old epitaph—

"What I gave I have,
What I spent I had,
What I kept I lost."

Which flatters thee with foolish dreams of
    night;
Curs'd is thy wasted bread, 80
Less lost, if dogs it fed;
At morn and eve thy tread
Was prompt to gather, and with both hands
    grip
What fleets so swiftly from thine ownership.

As wealth is gained without proportion due, 85
So is it without due proportion kept.
  This is it which hath swept
Many to bondage, and if one repent,
  'Tis not without great strife.
O Death, O Fortune, what is it ye do? 90
Why not set free the wealth which is not
    spent?
  If thus, for whom is't meant?
I know not; we within a sphere are swept
  Which ruleth all our life.
Reason that fails to check with faults is
    rife. 95
  Does he say, "I am bound"?
  What poor excuse is found
In this for ruler whom a slave commands!
  Nay, doubly base these bands,
If well ye mark where my hand shows the
    way. 100
False to yourselves, to others harsh, are ye,
  Who see men, wandering bare,
  O'er hills and marshes fare,

85-100 The bondage of the avaricious is the basest of all bondage. No one gets so little out of his wealth as he. He sees those of whom the world is not worthy wandering hungry and naked—(do we trace the feelings of the exile forced to "solicit the cold hand of charity" and to "solicit it in vain"? *Purg.* xi. 133-138; *Par.*

Men, before whom all vice hath fled away,
While ye heap rich robes on your mire and
clay. 105

The miser's eyes on purest virtue fall,
Virtue, who doth her foes to peace invite,
With lure full clear and bright
To draw them to her, but no good it brings,
For still he shuns the bait. 110
Then after many a turn and many a call,
The food to him, so great her care, she
flings,
Yet spreads he not his wings;
And if he comes when she hath vanished
quite,
His troubles seems as great 115
As if he gave not; so for him doth wait
No praise to kindness due:
I will that these my words be heard by you:
One with delay and one with vain parade,
And one with looks in shade, 120
Turns what he gives to bargain sold so dear,
As he knows only who such purchase pays.
Wilt know if his wound frays?
Who takes he so dismays,
Less bitter 'twere to meet a simple No: 125
And others and himself the miser woundeth
so.

xvii. 58)—and he clothes himself not even decently, but with vile apparel.

106-126 The sensitiveness of the poet shows itself again. He can tell how little the avaricious man cares for all the attractions by which Virtue seeks to win him; how he can mar even his gifts, such as they are, by a sourness or an ostentation that would make a refusal almost less bitter than the gift (*Purg*. xvii. 59; *Par*. xvii. 58-60). Even Can Grande's liberality may have been marred by his want of considerate sympathy. The imagery of ll. 109-113, reminds us of the similitudes from falconry in the *Commedia* (*H*. xvii. 127, xxii. 130; *Purg*. xix. 64; *Par*. xix. 34).

Thus, ladies, have I laid before you bare,
One limb of that vile race that looks on
you,
That wroth ye may them view.
But more unsightly still is that concealed, 130
Yea, far too foul to tell.
Of each 'tis true that each sin gathers there,
For friendship still in oneness is revealed;
And leaves that Love doth yield
Spring from the root of other blessing true; 135
Since like loves like indeed
Hear how to my conclusion I proceed;
Who to be fair doth deem
A good, must never dream
That she is loved indeed by such as these; 140
But if 'mong ills we please
To reckon beauty, she may trust it well,
Naming as love a brutal appetite.
May such dame perish quite
Who should her beauty bright 145
From natural goodness for such cause repel,
Nor deem love doth in Reason's garden
dwell!

Not far, my Canzon', doth a lady dwell,
Of our dear land the child,
Wise, beautiful, and mild; 150
All call on her, yet none may her discern:
When they her name would learn,
Bianca, Vanna, courteous calling her.

127-147 Nor is this all. As every virtue carries with it the seeds of other virtues, so the love of money is the root of all evil, and all other vices go with it; and the love of such a man is nothing better than a brute appetite. Woe for the woman who commits herself to such a man, and thinks that love is a plant which can grow elsewhere than in the garden of right reason. Witte rejects the closing stanza as spurious. A *v. l.* gives "*Giovane Contessa*" for "Gio-

Go thou thy way to her in meekness drest,
  There first thy course arrest; 155
  To her first manifest
Who thou art, and for what I bid thee stir;
Then at her hest be thou a follower.

CANZONE XIX

THE THREE EXILES

Tre donne intorno al cor mi son venute

Three ladies meet together round my heart,
  And sit outside its gate;
  Within, Love holds his state,
And lords it o'er my life with sovran sway:
So fair are they, and with such winning art, 5
  That this lord, strong and great,
  Who in my heart doth wait,

vanna, Cortese." We are in any case left to conjecture who "Bianca" was.

CANZONE XIX

The *Canzone* that follows takes its place among the noblest of Dante's lyrics, and deserves, perhaps, Fraticelli's praise as the noblest of all Italian poems of that form.

1-8 The three ladies that present themselves in the poet's vision have been differently identified as Justice, Generosity, and Temperance, or as the three forms of Righteousness, natural, political, and religious, or the Law of Nature, the Law of Moses, and the Law of Grace. I incline to the first interpretation. Rossetti, as might be expected, sees in them the Templars, the Albigenses, and the Ghibellines (*Spir. Antip.*, pp. 177-179); Keil, innocence, the love of God, and the love of man. The *Canzone*, it should be noted, names the first as Righteousness (*Drittura*); the others are not named, but are spoken of as respectively daughter and grand-

To tell of them scarce knoweth what to say.
Each one of them seems full of sore dismay,
Like one who is to weary exile borne, 10
  By this world left forlorn,
Whom nobleness and virtue nought avail.
  There was—so runs their tale—
A time when all men loved them and did
    bless,
Now with them all are wroth, or pass
    them by. 15
  So they, in loneliness,
Are come as those that do a friend's house
    seek,
For well they know he's there of whom I
    speak.

One mourns and wails in many a piteous tone,
  And on her hand doth pose, 20
  Like a dissevered rose;
Her naked arm, the pillar of her woe,
Feels the tear-gems that from her cheeks
    flow down;
  The other hand half hides
  The face where grief abides; 25
Unshod, unzoned, she still seems lady fair.
Soon as Love saw beneath the garment's tear

daughter of the first. This suggests the thought either (1) that generosity and temperance have their birth in justice, or (2) of the development and education of mankind by three successive manifestations in the Law of Nature, the Law of Moses, and the Law of Christ.

9-15 Comp. *Purg.* vi 88, xvi. 97, for a picture of like degeneracy.

27 The boldness of the imagery (comp. the same phrase in *Purg.* xxv. 43) startles us, but is, after all, Biblical (*Isai.* iii. 17; *Ezek.* xvi. 37). Men treat Righteousness or Purity, or whatever other virtue may be symbolised, as if she were the vilest object of their scorn. Love, however, looks on with wrath, and Righteousness claims him as her next of kin. Possibly there may be a reference to the myth that Astræa, the symbol of righteousness, was, like

That form whereof 'tis better not to speak,
He, wroth, yet pitying, meek,
Of herself questioned her, and that her woe. 30
"O thou, whom few do know,"
She answered, in a voice all choked with sighs,
"Our nature bids us that to thee we go.
I whose grief deepest lies,
Thy mother's sister, am named Righteousness, 35
How poor I am, let robes and zone confess."

When she had thus her name and state made known,
Great grief and shame inspired
My Lord, and he inquired
Who were the other two that with her came. 40
And she, who was to weep so ready shown,
Soon as his speech she heard,
To greater grief was stirred,
And said, "Dost thou for mine eyes feel no shame?"
And then began: "The Nile, as known to fame, 45

Venus, a daughter of Jupiter, or to the other mythos which made Nemesis and Diké the daughters of Themis.

45 We ask why Dante assigns to the second of the three virtues a birthplace near the sources of the Nile. Possibly it was thought of as the centre of the world's commerce, and therefore as the birthplace of the *jus gentium*. More probably the mediæval geography of Fazio degli Uberti (*Dittam.* v. 29) may throw some light on it. He describes those sources under the name Gion (the Gihon of *Gen.* ii. 13), and so the sources of the Nile are connected with the Earthly Paradise and with the natural virtues that belong to it. So in *Ecclus.* xxiv. 27, "Gehon" (Vulg., but "Nile" in Luther) is named as an ideal picture of the glories of Wisdom. The thought is therefore identical with that of *Purg.* i. 23. Men have abandoned the virtues of the Paradise life, and those virtues are strangers and pilgrims on the earth.

Forth from its fountain flows, a little stream,
There where the sun's hot beam
Robs the parched earth of willow's foliage
green;
By waters pure and clean
I brought her forth who standeth at my
side, 50
And with fair locks to dry her tears is seen;
And she, my child and pride,
Herself beholding in the fountain clear,
Brought forth the third who standeth not so
near."

Love paused awhile through sighs that from
him part, 55
And then with tender eyes,
Where erst wild thoughts did rise,
He greets the sisters three disconsolate.
And after taking of each kind a dart,
"Lift up your heads," he cries, 60
"Behold the arms I prize:
See how disuse their brightness doth abate.
Bounty and Temperance, and the rest
cognate
Of our high blood, must needs a-begging go;
Wherefore, if this be woe, 65
Let those eyes weep, those lips to wail it
learn,
Whom most it doth concern,
Who dwell beneath the rays of such a heaven;

62 Even Love's arrows, possibly the two arrows of gold and lead (*Ovid*), are blunted through long disuse. He has, however, the thought that he and the virtues who claim kinship with him are eternal. The two virtues named indicate an Aristotelian rather than a theological classification (Aristot. *Eth. Nic.* ii. 7; *Conv.* iv. 17). Men may suffer, but they remain, and they heed not the scorn of men. Comp. *H.* vii. 94.

Not ours, who to the eternal Rock may turn;
For, be we now sore driven, 70
We yet shall live, and yet shall find a race
Who with this dart shall each dark stain efface."

And I, who hear, as told in speech divine,
How exiles, great as these,
Are grieved, yet find some ease, 75
This my long banishment as honour hold;
And if man's judgment, or fate's ordered line,
Will that the world should learn
White flowers to black to turn,
To fall among the good with praise is told. 80
And but that I no more the star behold
Which, now far off removèd from my gaze,
Once burnt me with its blaze,
Light should I deem the burdens that oppress.
But this fire burns not less, 85
And has already eaten flesh and bone,
So that death's key upon my heart doth press.
Hence, though I guilt should own,
Many a month since that guilt is gone and spent,
If guilt but dieth soon as men repent. 90

69 That thought sustains the exiled poet. He too has his feet planted on the Rock of Ages. Though the white flowers may be turned to black (possibly, but only possibly, an allusive reference to the Bianchi, who were unfaithful to the ideal monarchy with which Dante had identified himself, and had joined the Guelph Neri, comp. *H.* ii. 128), yet he could glory in his loneliness and his sufferings (*Par.* xvii. 61-66). The sharpest pang was that he was still exiled from the city of his birth, which he loved with so passionate a love (*H.* xix. 47; *Par.* xxv. 1-9). Apparently that love led him to a hypothetical confession of his guilt, which stands in marked contrast to the well-known letter in which he refuses the humiliating conditions of the offered amnesty. The state of things implied seems to point to a time before 1309, when the hope of a return to Florence had become faint, and Henry VII. had not yet appeared on the scene to rekindle it.

My Song, let no man on thy robes lay hands,
To see what lady fair hides from all eyes:
Let parts unveiled suffice,
The sweeter fruit within to all deny,
To which hot hands draw nigh. 95
And if it chance that thou on one dost light
The friend of virtue, and to thee he cry,
Clothe thee in colours bright,
Then show thyself to him, that loving heart
May long for flower that shows so fair a
part. 100

CANZONE XX

LAUDES FLORENTIÆ

O patria, degna de trionfal fama

Dear country, worthy of triumphal fame,
Mother of high-souled sons,
Thy sister's grief thine own is far above:

91 The *Tornata* with which the *Canzone* ends seems to justify almost any amount of mystical interpretation, and so finds a parallel in *H.* ix. 61–63. Whether the meaning that lies below the surface is moral or political, whether the "friends of virtue" are those of spiritual discernment, who can discover a profound ethical significance, the secret beauty hidden from the eyes of the profane by the veil of symbolism, or a secret society of the Illuminati, Freemason, Carbonari type, readers will probably decide according to their theories. As elsewhere, I incline to the simpler, and, as it seems to me, more natural interpretation.

CANZONE XX

1. The "*patria*" is not Italy as a whole, but, as l. 3 shows, the city, the "sister of Rome," which was the poet's fatherland. The poem belongs obviously to his exile, but whether before or after

He, of thy children, feeleth grief and shame,—
Hearing what traitorous ones 5
Do in thee,—more, as he the more doth love.
Ah me, how prompt ill-doers are to move
In thee, for ever, plotting treachery,
With squint and envious eye,
Showing thy people still the false for true. 10
Lift up the sinking hearts, and warm their blood!
Upon the traitor's brood
Let judgment fall, that so with praises due
That grace may dwell in thee, which now complains,
Wherein all good is source and home attains. 15

Thou reigned'st happy in the fair past days,
When each that was thine heir
Sought that all virtues might thy pillars be;
Home of true peace and mother of all praise,
Thou in one faith sincere 20
Wert blest, and with the sisters four and three.
And now those fair forms have abandoned thee,
In mourning clad, with vices all o'erdone,
Thy true Fabricii gone:

Henry VII.'s campaign is open to conjecture. The tone is a little less bitter than that of *Purg*. vi. 145, or of the letter written to the Florentines after Henry had appeared on the scene.

II. The praises of the "good old times" remind us of *Par*. xv., xvi. The *seven ladies*, *i.e.*, the four cardinal virtues of natural ethics and the three supernatural graces, remind us of *Purg*. i. 23, xxxi. 103, 111, xxix. 121, and may so far point to the same period. So the reference to the "Fabricii" (who here stand for the Bianchi) finds a parallel in *Purg*. xx. 25. To punish in Antenôra (*H*. xxxii.

Haughty and vile, of true peace deadly foe; 25
Dishonoured one, hot faction mirroring still,
Since Mars thy soul doth fill;
Thou doom'st true souls to Antenôra's woe,
Who follow not the widowed lily's spear,
And those who love thee most have most to
fear. 30

Thin out that evil baleful root in thee,
Nor pity thou thy sons,
Who have thy fair flowers made all foul and
frail.
And wilt thou that the virtues victors be,
So that thy faithful ones, 35
Now hidden, rise with right, and sword in
hand,
Follow where still Justinian's beacons stand,
And thine unrighteous and revengeful laws
Correct, as wisdom draws,
That they may gain the praise of heaven
and earth. 40
Then with thy riches honour and endow
What sons best homage show,
Nor lavish them on those of little worth;
So that true Prudence and her sisters may
Dwell with thee still, nor thou disown their
sway. 45

88) is to treat as traitors. The "lily" of Florence is "widowed," not, as some have thought, because her chief leader, Corso Donati (?) or Philip the Fair (?), was dead, but because, like Israel, she had forsaken her true Lord, forgotten the "first love of her espousals" (*Jer.* ii. 2). *Lam.* i. 1 (quoted by Dante, *V. N.* c. 29; *Ep.* ix. 2) was still apparently in his thoughts.

III. The "flower" implies an allusive reference to the name *Fiorenza*. The name of Justinian, as in the magnificent episode of *Par.* vi. 1-90, is, for Dante, the symbol of wise and impartial legislation, standing out in marked contrast to the decree of banishment, forfeiture, attainder, death by burning, which had been passed, as before against the Uberti (*H.* x. 82-84), so more recently against

Serene and glorious, on the whirling sphere
Of every creature blest,
If thou dost this, thou shalt in honour reign,
And thy high name, which now with shame we hear,
On thee, Fiorenza, rest. 50
And soon as true affection thou shalt gain,
Blest shall the soul be, born in thy domain.
Thou wilt deserve all praise and majesty,
And the world's ensign be;
But if thy pilot thou refuse to change, 55
Then greater storms, and death predestinate
Expect thou, as thy fate;
And through thy paths all discords wild shall range.
Choose thou then now if peace of brotherhood
Or wolf-like ravin make most for thy good. 60

Dante and the Bianchi who were associated with him (*Purg.* vi. 110).

We note the pathos with which, in spite of all that he had suffered, the poet still clings to the city which he loved. Who could love her with so intense a love as his? Comp. *Par.* xxv. 1-9; *Conv.* i. 3. He will not give up the hope that she will yet welcome him back and crown him with honour.

IV. The words imply the thought of stellar influences, not, as in popular astrology, the result of blind chance or inexorable laws, but as guided by the angelic intelligences, who in their turn were under the control of the Divine Will which answered prayer, and made all things work together for good to those who loved Him. With this richness of blessing "Florence" would be at once *nomen et omen.* We note the parallelism of the closing lines with Henry VII.'s speech to the Italian delegates at Lausanne. What the "good ship" needed was a better pilot across the troubled sea of Italian politics, a pilot such as the Emperor or Dante himself might prove. Line 60 finds a parallel in *Par.* xxv. 6, and confirms the interpretation of *H.* i. 49, which sees in the "wolf" a symbol at once of avarice as such, and of Florence, as being, with the Papal Curia, its chief representative.

V. Even in Sodom there were ten righteous men. Even in Florence there were a few lights shining in the darkness (comp. *H.* vi. 73), such, *e.g.*, as Dino Compagni and Giovanni Villani; perhaps also the friend to whom *Ep.* 10 was addressed was perhaps in Dante's thoughts. He calls on them to come to the rescue of

Boldly and proudly now, my Canzon', go,
Since love thy steps doth guide;
Enter my land, for which I mourn and weep,
And thou wilt find some good men there, though low
Their light burns, nor spreads wide; 65
But they sink down, their virtues in the mire.
Cry to them, Rise, my trumpet bids aspire;
Take arms, and raise her to her place on high,
For she doth wasted lie.
For Capaneus and Crassus her devour, 70
Aglauros, Simon Magus, the false Greek,
And Mahomet, the weak
Of sight, who wields Jugurtha's, Pharaoh's power:
Then turn to her, good citizens and true,
And pray that she a nobler life renew. 75

his beloved fatherland. The names that follow recall passages in the *Commedia*. Crassus (*Purg*. xx. 116), Simon Magus (*H*. xix. 1; *Par*. xxx. 147), Capaneus (*H*. xiv. 63, xxv. 15), Aglauros (*Purg*. xiv. 139), the false Greek Sinon (*H*. xxx. 98), Mahomet (*H*. xxviii. 31). The names of Pharaoh and Jugurtha point to the regions of Egypt and Mauritania as under the rule of Islam.

SONNET XL

FRIENDLY WARNING

Io mi credea del tutto esser partit

I THOUGHT that I had parted evermore,
Good Messer Cino, from those rhymes of thine,
For now another course I must assign
To my good ship, already far from shore:
But since I hear it rumoured o'er and o'er 5
That thou art caught by any bait and line,
To give to this my pen I now incline,
A little while, my wearied fingers' lore.
Who falls in love, as is the case with thee,
Bound and set free by every new delight, 10
Shows that but lightly Love hath aimed his dart.
If to so many wills thy heart gives plight,
I pray in Heaven's name, it reformed may be,
That to your sweet words deeds be counterpart.

SONNET XL

The Sonnet is addressed to Guidoncino dei Sinibaldi, better known as Cino da Pistoia, one of Dante's early friends, the "poet of love," as he himself was the "poet of righteousness" (*V. E.* ii. 2). The parallelism of ll. 3, 4, with *Purg.* i. 1–3, seems to indicate that it was written in the later years of Dante's life. Other and higher work than that of writing sonnets has occupied his thoughts. As Cino returned to Pistoia in 1314, and was in exile when he answered Dante, the Sonnet must have been written before that date. Cino had apparently shown but little interest in his friend's graver work. Dante had heard, on his side, that Cino was no longer the true poet of love, faithful to the Selvaggia, who had been to him, in some measure, what Beatrice had been to Dante, but had transferred his devotion to another. Cynical critics, remembering the "*donna gentile*" of *V. N.* c. 36, the Gentucca of *Purg.* xxiv. 37, the "*Montanina*" of the letter to Moroello Malaspina might ask

SONNET XLI

QUIS LOCUS INGENIO?

Poich' io non trovo chi meco ragioni

SINCE I have none who will with me converse
  Of that Lord whom we serve, both you
      and I,
  Needs must I with the strong desire comply,
The good thoughts that stir in me to rehearse:
Naught else doth keep me in this mood per-
      verse   5
  Of silence that I feel so painfully,
  Save that my lot in such vile place doth lie,
That Good finds none to shelter it; yea, worse,

whether Dante was the man to cast the stone first at his friend's failings. On the other hand, however, it may be argued that a man, conscious that he was exposing himself to a retort, would hardly have written as Dante did, and so far the Sonnet takes its place as part of the evidence for the defence. Cino's answer (*Rim. Ant.* p. 340) is that he is in exile, a wanderer on the face of the earth, nigh unto death. He has not forsaken his first love, but he is banished from her, and finds joy in all beauty that resembles her. And as he finds that likeness in many fair ladies, that is the explanation of his apparent fickleness.

SONNET XLI

This also is addressed to Cino da Pistoia, and belongs to the period when both friends were in exile. Dante complains that where he is he finds none like-minded with himself. None know what true love is. This was the explanation of the poet's long silence. What the place was which he found so evil we are left to conjecture; probably Verona or Ravenna. The tone reminds us of *Par.* xvii. 58-60. Rossetti, *more suo*, finds a political meaning in the sonnet. Dante was in a Guelph city, and the "men" and the "ladies" of whom he speaks were the two orders of those who were initiated in the Ghibelline mysteries. On this theory "Love" is, of course, the Emperor, or, more probably, the ideal Empire (*Spir. Anti-Pap.* p. 156).

Love finds no home in face of lady fair,
Nor is there any man who for him sighs, 10
And were there one, "fool" would they call him there.
Ah! Messer Cino, ill our changed times fare:
To our great loss, and to our poesy's,
Since goodness such a scanty crop doth bear.

SONNET XLII

RIVALS OR PARTNERS

Due donne in cima della mente mia

Two ladies to the summit of my mind
Had come to hold discourse concerning love.
In virtue clothed and kindness, one doth move,
Prudence and honour follow close behind.

SONNET XLII

Among many other interpretations, of which I hardly need speak, the "two ladies" have been identified literally with Beatrice and the "*donna gentile*" of *V. N.* c. 36, mystically with the Theology and Philosophy whom they are supposed to represent. So interpreted, the Sonnet seems intended to reconcile the *Vita Nuova* and the *Convito*. I question the interpretation altogether, and find the key to the problem which the Sonnet presents in *Purg.* xxviii. and *Ball.* ii. and iii. The "lady" of the first quatrain is, I admit, Beatrice; but in the other I find Matilda. Here also there is the *leggiadria*, the "gaiety," the "gentleness," the "virtue," of which we read in *Ball.* iii. And with it there is joined the high and noble activity of which Matilda is the admitted symbol (*Purg.* xxviii. 40, *n.*). So understood, the lines throw light, if I mistake not, both on the outward and inward life of Dante. He had loved both Beatrice and Matilda with a pure and ardent love in his early youth

Beauty the other hath and grace refined, 5
And a fresh honour gentleness doth prove;
And I, by grace of my dear Lord above,
Do homage to their sovereignty combined.
Beauty and virtue both the soul invite,
And question, Can a heart, in loyalty 10
Of perfect love, to ladies twain be plight?
The fount of gentle utterance makes reply,
"Yea, Beauty may be loved for her delight,
And Virtue likewise for her workings high."

SONNET XLIII

FAIR BUT CRUEL

Nulla mi parrà mai più crudel cosa

Nought can to me more pitiless appear
Than she, to serve whom I my life have lost,
For her affection is as lake in frost,
And mine dwells ever in Love's furnace clear.

(*V. N.* c. 8). He loved their transfigured memories in his manhood and his age. He loved with an almost equal love the active and contemplative life, which they respectively represented. Like another Jacob, he could love both Leah and Rachel, and, in his case, neither would be jealous of the other, and each, as in *Purg.* xxviii.-xxxiii., would do her part in leading him to Lethe and Eunoe, to the oblivion of all evil, and the revival of all good memories, as the condition of his attaining to completeness.

SONNET XLIII

Apparently a reproduction in verse of the thought of *Conv.* iii. 11-15. Wisdom, as in the Assisi fresco, has turned her severer aspect towards her worshipper. The "frozen lake" reminds us of *H.* xxxiv. 22-24; the "fire of love," of the well-known hymn of

Of this fair maid, so proud and so severe, 5
I joy to see the beauty she doth boast,
And so with love of my great pain am tost,
No other pleasure to my eye comes near.
Not she, who ever turns the Sun to see,
And, changed herself, a love unchanged doth keep, 10
Had ever, as I have, a woe so deep;
Therefore, since never can thy full power sweep
O'er this fair proud one, Love, ere life shall flee,
For pity's sake, come, sigh awhile with me.

SONNET XLIV

FAITH AND UNFAITH

Lo re, che merta i suoi servi a ristoro

The king, who doth his servants recompense
In fullest measure, heaped and running o'er,
Bids me my rancorous pride indulge no more,
And to the highest Council look from hence:

St. Francis of Assisi; l. 9 refers to the story of Clytie (*Met.* iv. 270), who loved Apollo, and was turned into a sunflower, so that she might always gaze on him. "*Vertitur ad solem, mutataque servat amorem.*" It is noticeable that this and the following Sonnet are addressed in the Ambrosian MSS. to a Giovanni Quirino, a poet of Venice. Poems bearing that name are found in the MS. from which this Sonnet is taken in the Ambrosian Library at Milan.

SONNET XLIV

The "dear friend" to whom the Sonnet is addressed is the Giovanni Quirino just named (*S.* 43, *n.*). The thoughts and language alike point to the time when Dante was finishing the *Paradise.* In the Ambrosian MS. it comes as an answer to one in which the

And thinking on the choir of citizens, 5
Who in the heavenly city evermore
Praise their Creator, I, a creature, soar,
Eager to praise yet more His love immense.
For if the future prize I contemplate,
To which God calls all born of Christian race, 10
Nought else can in my wishes find a place.
But much I mourn for thee, dear friend,
whose face
Turns not to look upon that future state,
Losing sure good for shows that hope frustrate.

BALLATA XI

THE BEATIFIC VISION

Poichè saziar non posso gli occhi miei

Since still I fail mine eyes to satisfy,
With looking on my lady's face so fair,
So fixed my glances there
Shall be, that bliss shall spring from seeing her.

writer congratulates Dante on the work he had accomplished in honour of God and of the Virgin, but speaks mournfully of himself, as being without hope, either for this world or the life to come, in the tone of an epicurean who lives on, though life is no longer for him worth living. Dante, in his reply, speaks in far different tones. He has laid aside the bitterness of past years. He gazes on the heavenly Consistory (*Par.* xxix. 67), on the citizens of the holy city (*Par.* xxxi., xxxii.). He finds strength and comfort in the hope of the great reward. He can but mourn that his friend is not a sharer in that hope.

BALLATA XI

The evidence of authorship is not certain, the poem being found in some MSS. as written by Cino of Pistoia. It is, however,

E'en as an angel who in essence pure 5
Doth still on high endure,
And seeing God, in fullest bliss hath part:
Thus mortal, and no more,
Beholding the full store
Of beauty in her face who holds my heart, 10
I too of blessedness may learn the art.
Such is her virtue that it spreads and flows,
Though what it is none knows,
Save him whose yearnings honour true confer.

BALLATA XII

SPRING-TIDE JOY

Fresca rosa novella

FRESH rose, just newly born,
And joy-inspiring Spring,
As I in gladness sing,
Through meadow and by stream,
How high I you esteem 5
I tell each green plantation.

received by Fraticelli, Krafft, and Witte. The thought seems to me sufficiently Dantesque. The bliss of the saints consists, as throughout the *Paradiso*, in the beatific vision of God : so the lover finds his joy in the vision of the beloved one. Here, as elsewhere, we ask who was present to the poet's thoughts, Beatrice in the flesh, or as transfigured into Divine Wisdom or Philosophy, or some earthly *pargoletta*. Probably here, as elsewhere, the first two answers would both be true, melting into each other like dissolving views.

BALLATA XII

We are once more in a region of conjecture. The poem has been

Yes, your high praise shall flow,
In joy renewed by all,
The great ones and the small,
Whatever path they go; 10
And birds shall trill their call
Each in the tongue they know,
In eve or morning's glow,
On the green shrubs and tall:
And all the world shall sing 15
(As is indeed most meet),
Since cometh spring-tide sweet,
Your high praise and glory,
Telling out your story,
Your angel-like creation. 20

Angelic beauty shining
In thee, Lady, showeth.
Heaven! what joy he knoweth
Who for thee was pining!
Thy face, where true joy gloweth, 25
Since far behind it leaveth
All that use perceiveth,
Still in wonder groweth.

ascribed to Enzo, king of Sardinia, son of Frederick II., and to Guido Cavalcanti; to the latter chiefly on the strength of the fact that the "*primavera*" (=spring) in l. 2 is supposed to allude to the mistress of his affections, who was known by that name (*V. N.* c. 24). In tone and form the poem approximates more closely to the love-poems of Provençal literature than any of the poems recognised without dispute as Dante's. On any assumption, I find it hard to connect it with any definite fact in Dante's life, and am inclined to look on it, assuming that he wrote it, as being, like the three *Sestinas*, one of the metrical experiments by which he sought to perfect his mastery over all forms of versification.

12 The use of the word *latino* in the original for the song of birds may be noted as specially characteristic of the early Italian and Provençal poets, notably of Dante's favourite, Arnauld Daniel (Witte). In *Par.* iii. 63 it is used for "clear speech" generally.

Goddess-like 'mong women,
As thou art, thou seemest, 30
With such beauty gleamest,
That 'tis past my telling,
Past Nature's power, excelling
E'en all imagination.

Yes, beyond man's nature, 35
Thy most beauteous presence,
God has made as essence
Of each fairest creature;
On me may that grace shine,
Nor far from me abide 40
The will of God benign!
And if it seem too daring
That I to love am driven,
Well may I yet be shriven;
For love my soul assaileth, 45
With whom nor strength availeth
Nor Reason's moderation.

SONNET XLV

WHAT IS LOVE?

Molti, volendo dir che fosse Amore

MANY who fain would tell what Love may be
  Have spoken words enough, yet failed they still
  To say of him what half the truth should fill,
Or note of his high greatness the degree:
And one there was who in it heat did see   5
  Of soul, through which the thoughts of fancy
    thrill;
  And others said that 'twas desire of will,
Born of the heart in joyous ecstasy.
But I affirm Love hath no substance true,
  Nor is corporeal thing with shape imprest,   10
Rather is it a passion, strong to woo,
  Delight in beauty, gift by Nature blest,
So that the heart nought other doth pursue,
  And this suffices, while in joy we rest.

SONNET XLV

Fraticelli places this *Sonnet* among the doubtful poems; Witte accepts it; Krafft leaves it as an open question. The question mooted in it is discussed with some fulness in the *V. N.* (c. 20), where the solution of the problem is that Love is not in itself a substance, but the accident of a substance. Line 5 seems to refer to a Sonnet by Jacopo da Lentino, the Notary of *Purg.* xxiv. 56 (*Rim. Ant.* p. 318)—

"*Amor è un desio, che vien dal core*
Per l' abbondanza del gran piacimento."

"Love is desire, which springeth from the heart
Through great abundance of exceeding joy."

An apparent allusion to this Sonnet in the *Acerba* of Cecco d'Ascoli suggests the inference that it was addressed to Cino of Pistoia.

SONNET XLVI

SPRING AFTER WINTER

Ora che'l mondo s' adorna e si veste

Now that the world hath donned her bright array
Of leaves and flowers, and smiles clothe every field,
And cold and cloud to skies of brightness yield,
And living creatures all are glad and gay:
And each one seems to own Love's gentle sway, [5]
And small birds, singing from their throats unsealed,
Leave off the cries where tones of wailing pealed,
And pour on hills and vales and woods their lay:
Now that the season, sweet, and glad, and clear,
Of spring doth come in its own verdure clad, [10]
My hope revives, and I once more am glad,
As one who life and praise hath ever had
From that dear Lord, above all others dear,
Who gives to me, his slave, no grudging cheer.

SONNET XLVI

The discovery of the *Sonnet* is due to Witte, who disinterred it from the Ambrosian MS. Fraticelli thinks its authorship doubtful. It seems intended to be a complement to *Canz*. xi., representing the revival of the lover's hope under the sweet influences of spring as that did the survival of his passion under the benumbing frosts of winter. The last words of the *Canzone* seem to promise such a complement. In the one, as in the other, it is open to us to find both a literal and an allegorical meaning. The poet's passion may be that for Beatrice, or the *donna gentile*, or Philosophy.

SONNET XLVII

GOLD TRIED IN THE FIRE

Per villania di villana persona

THROUGH baseness uttered by the base in mind,
Or through the whisper of the vile and rude,
It is not meet that lady wise and good,
Around whose brows the wreaths of praise are twined,
Should grieve, or deem that fair fame twice refined, 5
Which is throughout with clearest light imbued,
Can thus be lost; by her 'tis understood
That truth 'gainst her no cause of fault can find.
As is the rose among the brambles seen,
Or in the fiery furnace purest gold, 10
So thee, where'er thou art, may men behold.
Let then the fools prate on with tongue o'erbold,
For well 'tis known, thou greater praise dost glean
Than if such wretches' speech had fairer been.

SONNET XLVII

This, like the preceding *Sonnet*, was published by Witte from the Ambrosian MS.; is accepted by him; rejected by Krafft; placed by Fraticelli among the doubtful poems. To me it seems not unworthy of Dante, and may possibly connect itself with the passage in the *Vita Nuova* (c. 5, 9), in which he says that the poems which he addressed ostensibly to one of the ladies of Florence whom he chose as a "screen" for his passion for Beatrice, gave occasion to the gossip of the scandalmongers (*V. N.* c. 12). In substance it is an application of the converse of the "*laudari a laudato*" maxim. It reminds us of the "*lascia dir le genti*" of *Purg.* v. 13, and of

"To be dispraised of some is no small praise."

SONNET XLVIII

AD MISERICORDIAM

Poichè, sguardando, il cor feriste in tanto

SINCE with thy glance thou so hast pierced my heart
With sharpest stroke, that it is nigh to bleed
For pity's sake some slight respite concede,
That my sad spirit may not all depart:
Dost thou not see mine eyes with weeping smart, 5
Still grieving so for sorrows that exceed,
Which still my footsteps to death's confines lead,
That I no refuge find in any part?
Behold and see, O Lady! if I mourn,
And if my voice hath passed to thinnest tone, 10
While still to thee love's suppliant sighs are borne,
And if it please thee, Lady dear, mine own,
That this my heart with sorrow should be worn,
Yet still am I thy humblest servant known.

SONNET XLVIII

What has been said of *Sonnets* xlvi., xlvii., applies to this *Sonnet* also, save that Krafft admits its genuineness. Lines 5-7 present a parallel with *Canz.* vi. 1-3. In the Italian the verbs in ll. 1 and 9 are in the plural, those in ll. 3 and 5 in the singular, the former being addressed to the lady of the poet's love, the latter to God.

SONNET XLIX

STRENGTH IN WEAKNESS

Togliete via le vostre porte omai

"Throw open wide your gates in all men's
sight,
And she shall enter who doth others raise,
For she is one in whom dwells lasting praise,
And full of courage is, and great in might."
"Ah me! Alas!"—"What means this doleful
plight?"— 5
"I tremble so, that no strength with me
stays."
"Take heart, for I will be to thee always
A help and life, as thou shalt tell aright."
"Nay, I feel all my strength as bound in thrall
Of secret virtue that with her she brings, 10
And I see Love who threatens fearful
things."
"Turn thee to me, for in me joy upsprings;
And let the strokes behind thee only fall;
Nor fear; soon will they vanish, one and all."

SONNET XLIX

Found in the Ambrosian and one other MS. as Dante's; accepted by Witte; doubted by Fraticelli. There are apparently three interlocutors in the dialogue. Love bids the poet open the gates of his soul, that the lady whom he loves may enter. He, however, shrinks once and again in the consciousness of his weakness (comp. *V. N.* c. 2), till the beloved one herself interposes, as in l. 12, to reassure him. Here once more letter and allegory probably interpenetrate. The beloved one may be Beatrice or Philosophy.

CANZONIERE

CANZONE XXI

IN MEMORIAM

Poscia ch' i' ho perduta ogni speranza

SINCE every hope of mine hath from me gone,
 Thy face again, my Lady fair, to see,
  Nought is there, nor can be,
 To comfort me in this my bitterness.

CANZONE XXI

1 The judgments of Dante experts are divided as to the authenticity of this *Canzone*. Witte (*Lyr. Ged.*, p. 159) receives it on the strength of its having been published as Dante's in the Venice edition of 1518, and of its appearing in one or two MSS. with his name attached to it. He is followed by Fauriel (*Dante*, i. p. 233) and Blanc. To them the style seems sufficiently on Dante's level, and the facts which the poem implies to fit in with the records of Dante's life. Fraticelli, on the other hand, rejects it (*O. M.* i. pp. 298-305) on the ground that it is wanting in many printed editions of the *Canzoniere*, and in the greater number of the MSS. of Dante's minor poems; that the style is too weak and diffuse to be recognised as his, and that the facts do not fit in with what is known of Dante's later years after the death of Henry VII. Krafft (*Lyr. Ged.* pp. 460-464) and Trivulzio (quoted in *Frat. O. M.* i. p. 304) agree with him in this judgment. The last-named critic is disposed to assign it to Dante's friend, Cino da Pistoia; Fraticelli to a friend of Petrarch's, Senuccio Benuccio, who appears as the author in some MSS. It is difficult to speak positively in such a case, but I incline, on the whole, with Witte, to accept the *Canzone* as authentic, and have therefore included it in my translation. It has, at any rate, the interest of being the expression of a sorrow which, if not Dante's own, was at least, that of one like-minded with himself, springing from the event which overthrew his hopes for himself and for the city which he loved with a passionate enthusiasm. The notes which follow will naturally deal with the internal evidence on the strength of which the poem has been accepted or rejected by the critics I have named.

2 The "Lady fair" is identified by Witte with Florence. Fraticelli asserts that this is not after Dante's manner, but the opening lines of *Canz.* xx. present a sufficient parallel. The whole passage reminds us of the first stanza of *Canz.* vii., though there, of course, he speaks of the personal Beatrice.

To look on thee again hope have I none, 5
For Fate hath stopped the way that leads to
thee,
By which, perchance, for me
Had been return to thy high nobleness.
Therefore my heart abides in such distress,
That I consume myself in sighs and tears, 10
Waiting the many years
I bide, and yet my life Death quenches not.
What shall I do? Love still on me doth
press,
And failing hope on every side appears,
No vesture safety bears, 15
Or succour, all brings torment as my lot,
Save only that I call on Death to slay,
And every life-pulse loudly calls alway.

That hope of mine, which whilome led me far
From thy fair charms, which charm me more
and more, 20
I now as false deplore,
Made false by Death, of every good the foe;
For Love, through whom thy hands trium-
phant are,
Had promised strength and peace on me to
pour.
Through wise and truthful lore 25

6 The thought implied is that the success of Henry VII.'s enterprise might have opened the way to an honourable return to Florence, which on its failure was closed to him, except on conditions which, as in *Ep.* x., it was impossible for him to accept.

17 We are again reminded of *Canz.* vii. (ll. 16–20).

19 The poet's hope in Henry of Luxemburg had led him to reject all other means of returning to Florence. The subject-matter of the poem led him to dwell on that hope as the reason of his absence, rather than on the fact that the city had banished him. That hope the Emperor's death had frustrated, yet he could not regret that he had followed one who was so worthy of all honour. Line 22 reminds

He my soul strengthened, poor and full of
woe,
And led me labours sweet, though hard, to
know:
He made me part from thee for honour's sake,
Wishful for thee to take
My way, to win more fame and high estate. 30
My lord I followed: should one say me "No"
When I proclaim him noblest lord on earth,
That "No" in lies hath birth;
For never was there one so good and great,
Wise, temperate, brave, and largely liberal, 35
More just than doth to lot of mortals fall.

This lord, by God's own justice fashionèd
For virtue, of all men that are, elect,
Used with supreme effect
His power, far more than any erst had done. 40
By neither pride nor avarice was he led,
Nor fortune ill in him revealed defect;
For still one might detect
The strength which, dauntless, bade his foes
come on.
Wherefore by right and good choice was I
won 45

us of *Ball.* ii. 1, and the estimate of Henry's character of *Par.* xxx. 136, and *Epp.* v. 2, vii. 2.

35 Witte quotes a parallel from an unpublished canzone ascribed in some MSS. to Dante—

"*Questo magnificente, ver, giocondo,*
Magnanimo, affabile, gentile." . . .

38 The words find a striking parallel in *Ep.* v. 1–5. Henry was, in Dante's thoughts, the divinely chosen ruler who realised the ideal of the *De Mon.*

41.42 Comp. the picture of the ideal deliverer in *H.* i. 103. Witte quotes another parallel from the canzone thus named—

"*Alla impresa manifesta il vero*
Ancora che gli 'l contrarii la ventura.

In retinue of lord so dear to stay;
And if such went astray
Who strove against his might with all their power,
I might not with their hosts of falsehood run.
I went with him, and shunned his foes alway, 50
Nor should we pine away,
Though Death hath turned the sweet cup into sour;
For men should still do good because 'tis good,
Nor can he fail who doeth what he should.

Some are there who but use for wealth and praise 55
The goods which they to Nature's bounty owe;
Whence little heed, I trow,
They take how they their life may rightly lead.
The honour others give no worth displays;
But honour which a man in act doth show, 60
As righteous uses grow,
That is his very own, and praised his deed.
How were such glory then as nought decreed
When Death a lord so loved and honoured slew?
No true soul takes that view, 65
Nor healthy thought, nor soul with vision clear.

47 Comp. *Ep.* v. 4, in which Dante reproaches the Italian princes for resisting the ordinance of God in rejecting Henry's sovereignty.
56-63 Almost a *replica* of *Canz.* xvi. 21-40, on true nobility.

O saintly soul, raised to thy heavenly meed,
Subject and foe alike thy loss might rue,
Did but this world pursue
Its course as ruled by men who good
revere,— 70
Rue his own guilt, who from thee failed and
fell,—
Rue his own life, who loved and followed well.

I wail my life, for thou, my lord, art dead;
More than I love myself did I love thee,
In whom was hope for me 75
Of home-return, where I should be content.
And now, with all that hope of comfort fled,
More than all else, my life goes heavily.
Death, stern and harsh to see,
How hast thou ta'en from me the sweet in-
tent, 80
Once more to see the fairest pleasures blent,
That e'er the power of Nature brought to
birth
In lady of great worth,
Whose beauty is so full of holiest grace!
This thou hast taken from me, and assigned 85
Such sorrow as men never know on earth;
For now, in life-long dearth,
I have no hope to see the much-loved face;
For he is dead, and I am far off still,
And therefore hopeless sorrow works its
will. 90

80-86 The critics who reject Dante's authorship lay stress on the inconsistency between this language and the bitterness with which he speaks of the Florentines in *Ep.* vi. and generally throughout the *Commedia*; aud Trivulzio assumes, on the supposition that the *Canzone* was written by Cino de Pistoia, that the lady who is thus praised was one of flesh and blood, Selvaggia, or another, whom the poet had hoped to see on returning to his native city. I own that

My song, thou journeyest into Tuscan land,
To that great joy above all others dear;
End then thy journey there,
Telling in words of woe my sad estate.
But, ere thou pass from Lunigiana's strand, 95
To Marquis Franceschino draw thou near,
And, with thy sweet speech clear,
Tell him some hope in him with me doth wait;
And since my distance from him sore doth grieve,
Pray him that I his answer may receive. 100

I do not see the alleged incompatibility. Dante's burning indignation against the citizens of Florence might well co-exist, as *Par.* xxv. 1-9 shows that it did, with a passionate affection for the city of his birth, with an equally passionate eagerness to end his days there, if that were possible, as it had once seemed possible, consistently with his self-respect.

94 The *envoi* of the *Canzone* has furnished arguments for the adverse critics. If it had to pass through the Lunigiana on its way to Tuscany, it must, they urge, have been sent from France or Provence, or at least Liguria or Lombardy, and we have no record of Dante's presence in any of those regions till we find him in 1317 with Can Grande at Verona. It is, I think, a sufficient answer to this objection to say, that the very incompleteness of our knowledge of Dante's wanderings after the death of Henry VII., admits the possibility of a visit to Verona or to Brescia, where Moroello Malaspina had been appointed by Henry as Imperial vicar. Dante, as *Purg.* viii. 121-132 shows, was largely indebted to the friendship and hospitality of the whole family, and the Franceschino who is here named was named with him as procurator in the negotiation of the treaty of Sarzana (1306), between the Malaspina family and the Bishop of Luni. So far as I know, there was no like connection between that family and either of the two other poets to whom the *Canzone* has been conjecturally ascribed.

CANZONIERE

DANTE'S CONFESSION OF FAITH

I. CREDO

FULL oft have I of Love writ many rhymes,
As sweet and fair and pleasant as I might,
And much have sought to polish them betimes;
But now my every wish is altered quite,
Because I know that I have spent in vain 5
My labours, and scant wage may claim of right.
From that false Love I now my hand restrain;
The pen that wrote of him aside being laid,
And, as a Christian, speak of God full plain.

It is not without a certain measure of hesitation that I have decided on translating and publishing the series of didactic poems that follow. I must own that I do not find in them the traces of the master's hand. The narrative which introduces them is suspiciously defective as to date and place. It comes to us through an anonymous MS. (1011 in the Bibl. Riccardiana of Florence); is not mentioned by Boccaccio, or any of the earlier commentators on the *Commedia*. On the other hand, it is received by Fraticelli, Witte, and Krafft, and included by the two latter in their translations of Dante's Minor Poems. The tradition connected with it has a certain biographical interest. The poems themselves represent fairly enough the current theology and ethics of the Latin Church of the 13th and 14th centuries, and thus serve to throw light on Dante's teaching. And so the scale was turned in favour of translating, and the reader can exercise his own judgment. I begin with epitomising the tradition to which I have referred.

After the *Commedia* was published, it was studied by many theologians, among others by those of the Franciscan Order. They read in *Par.* xi. 121–139 the lamentations of St. Francis over the degeneracy of his Order, and the poet's own words as to that degeneracy. They were irritated, and set to work to see if they could find materials in his book for accusing him of heresy. He was brought before the Inquisitor on that charge. He asked for a short respite to prepare his defence. It was then past vespers (6 P.M.). By 9 A.M. next day he appeared with his Profession of Faith, written during the night, in the same metre as the *Commedia*. As soon as the Inquisitor had read it, with twelve masters in theology

I. In God the Father I believe, Who made [10]
All things that are, from Whom all good doth flow
That is through all their varied forms displayed.
II. Through heaven and earth His grace still worketh so,
And out of nothing He created all,
Perfect, serene, and bright with beauty's glow. [15]

as his assessors, who were unable to find heresy in it, he pronounced a sentence of acquittal, and dismissed the accusers with a reprimand.

I own that the story reminds me overmuch of Defoe's Introduction to Drelincourt on *Death*, and I see in it something like a pious fraud, the object of which was to gain the sanction of a great name for an edifying manual of faith and devotion. The *Dittamondo* of Fazio degli Uberti shows that the form of the *terza rima* soon attracted many imitators, and I take the writer of these poems to have been one of them. Possibly also—for the motives of the writers of *apocrypha* are often manifold—he may have thought he was doing something to vindicate the fair fame of Dante against the charge of heresy. It will be remembered that the *De Monarchiâ* had been condemned and burnt as heretical by the Cardinal del Poggetto, with the authority of Pope John XXII., after Dante's death (Bocc. *V. D.* p. 259, ed. 1733).

With regard to the paraphrase of the Seven Penitential Psalms in *terza rima*, which are commonly printed with the Profession of Faith, there seemed to me to be even less reason for entering on the work of a translator. I do not find any adequate evidence, external or internal, of their genuineness. They present no special points of interest in connection with Dante's acknowledged work, or with the belief of the Mediæval Church, and without such points of contact a translation of a translation of yet another translation has but little chance of being more than a weak dilution of the original.

The reader will hardly, I think, be surprised that, with this view of the characters of the poems, I have thought it best to minimise my work as a commentator. I have not thought it necessary to give scriptural proofs of the doctrines asserted in the *Credo*, or to point out how the *pseudo* (I can scarcely say the *deutero*) Dante, by following in the footsteps of the Church's Creeds, avoids the errors of Ebion and Cerinthus, of Arius and Sabellius, of Nestorius and Eutyches. The writer apparently knows nothing of the *Commedia*, and yet the tradition which introduces the Paraphrase makes that the starting-point of the charge of heresy. Would it not have been enough, one asks, to refer to the poet's examination by the three great Apostles in *Paradise* if it had been necessary to vindicate its orthodoxy? And further, the writer thinks of the

III. Both things that under sight, touch, hearing, fall,
Were fashioned by His goodness infinite,
And those which we things intellectual call.

IV. And I believe the Son did flesh unite,
Man's flesh and life, in womb of Virgin blest, 20
Who helps us with her prayers by day and night:
And that the Godhead's glory thus did rest
On Christ, in all His sinless holiness,
As holy Church doth in her praise attest.

V. Him thus we perfect God and man confess, 25
The only Son of God, eternally
Begotten, God of God, whose Name we bless:

VI. Begotten, not created, God most High,
Like to the Father, with the Father One,
And with the Holy Ghost; mysteriously 30

VII. Incarnate, Who that He might all atone,
Upon the holy Cross was crucified,
Not for His fault, but of free grace alone.
Then did He pass to that pit deep and wide
Of darkness that He might the souls set free 35
Of the old fathers that did there abide,

Dante whom he personates only as the author of the poems of the *Vita Nuova*, and those poems simply amatory. The allegorical significance of the "*donna gentile*" as one with Philosophy, of the idealised Beatrice as one with Theology, is clearly unknown to him even by report. He puts into Dante's lips a confession like that which we find in Chaucer's *Persone's Tale*, that also being probably the pious fraud of a personated authorship.

17 Comp. the inference of *H.* iii. 1–9 as deduced from the received dogmas of the Church. If Hell be part of God's creation, it must owe its origin to Supreme Goodness as well as to Supreme Power.

35 We note the mediæval views of the Descent into Hades as seen in *H.* iv. 52-60.

With watching hearts, till God and man
should be
United, and throw wide their prison
door,
And by His passion give them liberty.
Certain it is that who holds this true lore 40
Complete, and with unswerving fealty,
Is through that Passion saved for ever-
more.
And him who doubteth this, or doth deny,
As heretic we blame, his own worst foe,
Losing his soul that doth not this
descry. 45

VIII. From the Cross taken, in the grave laid low,
On the third day, with body and with
soul,
He rose again, as we believe and know.

IX. And with the self-same flesh, complete and
whole,
He took from her, the Virgin Mother
blest, 50
He soared on high beyond the starry
pole;

X. And sits, and shares the Eternal Father's
rest,
Till He shall come to judge the quick
and dead,
And recompense them both with interest.
Wherefore let each man's work of good be
sped, 55
And for good deeds let him hope
Paradise,
Where God's grace shall on us His heirs
be shed.

55 The Paraphrase of the Creeds, like the Creeds themselves,

And he who sunk in sin and vices lies,
Let him expect in Hell all grief and pain,
Sharing with demons their dread miseries. 60
And of these woes no respite may he gain,
For they unchanging last for evermore,
And cries of anguish pour their ceaseless strain.

XI. From such a doom may He whom we adore,
The Holy Spirit, save poor souls undone, 65
Third Person, where is neither less nor more.
For as the Father is, such is the Son,
And such the Holy Spirit equally,
One God, and of three Holies, Holy One.
Such is in truth the Blessed Trinity, 70
That Son and Father, equally divine,
Are with the Spirit One mysteriously;
From this desire and love, as both combine,
Proceeding, from the Father and the Son,
Not made nor yet begotten—this Creed's mine. 75

XII. He from that Love and Purpose high alone,
Of Son and Father doth proceed and reign,
Nor this nor that as single source doth own.
Who so attempts more subtly to explain
What the full Being of our God may be, 80
Wastes all his labour, and his toil is vain.

ignores the doctrine of *Purgatory*, which occupies so prominent a place in the *Commedia*.

XIII. Alone let it suffice that firmly we
Believe in that which Holy Church doth teach,
Who thereof giveth us the true decree.

SACRAMENTA

I. Baptism, I do believe, adorneth each [85]
With grace divine and makes him wholly clean
Of sin, and doth to every virtue reach:
The fruit of water and the word is here,
Nor more than once is it to any given,
Though he from deadly sin return in fear. [90]
And failing this, all hope from each is riven
Of passing onward to the life eterne,
Although he own all virtues under Heaven.
Light of that lamp that doth so brightly burn,
From the blest Spirit oft in us doth show, [95]
And all our wishes in the right way turn,
For keen desire for Baptism burneth so
In us, that for his right volition still,
No less than deed, the righteous man we know.

[85] *Accedit verbum ad elementa et fit sacramentum* was the definition of mediæval theology. From the Creed we pass to an account of the Seven Sacraments of the Latin Church, Baptism, Penance, the Eucharist, Ordination, Confirmation (the Chrism of l. 143), Extreme Unction, Matrimony. The order in which they are named is not that of theological systems. Possibly the necessities of rhyme may have led to the variation.

II. And to cleanse us from our unrighteous
will, 100
And from the sins that from God
separate,
We Penance have for wholesome
chastening still;
III. Nor by our power, nor skill, however great,
Can we return to win God's bounteous
grace,
Unless Confession comes to renovate. 105
This first involves contrition to efface
Ills thou hast done, with thine own
mouth then speed
To own the sin that works in us apace.
Then Satisfaction we, as next stage, reach,
Which with the acts aforesaid doth
unite, 110
Used well, to win the pardon we
beseech.
IV. But since our evil foe doth still incite
Our weak will unto wrong, to our great
woe,
And little fears our virtue's vaunted
might
That we may 'scape the fraud that cruel
foe 115
Still ever plans our weakness to ensnare,
E'en he from whom all world-wide evils
flow,—
Our Lord and God doth in His love
prepare,
Father and Friend, Christ's Body and
His Blood,
And on the altar shows them to us
there, 120

His own dear Body, which upon the wood
Of the blest Cross hung, and Its blood there shed
To liberate us from the foul fiend's brood.
And if, apart from error, truth be read,
We see the very Christ, the Virgin's Son 125
Veiled in the Host beneath the form of bread,
True God commingled with true Man in One,
Beneath that outward show of bread and wine,
That gift by which our Paradise is won.
So great and holy, wondrous and divine, 130
Is that mysterious awful sacrament,
That my best speech the truth may not define.
This gives us boldness, gives encouragement,
Against the cunning tempter's subtlest art,
So that his skill on us is vainly spent; 135
For there God hears the pleadings of our heart,
Which flow from fervent faith in love intense,
And from sincere contrition take their start.
The power to work this miracle immense,
To sing the hours, and others to baptise, 140
These gifts of might priests only may dispense.

v.vi. And to confirm our Christian mysteries,
We chrisma and the holy oil possess,
Through which our faith gains stronger energies.

vii. Our flesh, which evermore to sin doth press, 145
Its pulses stirred by sensual appetite,
Oft prompts to deeds of foul lasciviousness.
To check this evil God, in wise foresight,
Appointed Marriage as a remedy,
So that this sin might lose its baneful might. 150
And thus from Satan's snare that we may fly,
The seven blest sacraments a way provide,
With prayers and alms and fasts continually.

DECALOGUS

i. Ten great Commandments God has given as guide,
The first that we should worship Him alone, 155
Nor to false gods and idols turn aside.

ii. Nor to His holy Name should wrong be done,
Or by false swearing, or by deed unblest,
But ever should we bless the Holy One.

155 As in the received arrangement of the Latin Church, what we know as the Second Commandment is incorporated with the First. The position given to the Sixth, as coming between the Ninth and Tenth, has, so far as I know, no authority. The division of the

III. The third that we should from all labour
        rest   160
    On one day of the week, the Lord's
        own day,
    As in the Church's law is manifest.
IV. And 'tis His will that we should duly pay
    To Father and to Mother reverence
        meek,
    Since we from them derive our mortal
        clay.   165
V. VI. No wrong on life or goods of others wreak,
VII. But chastely live, in stainless purity,
    Nor shame for others nor dishonour
        seek.
VIII. For naught of good we find beneath the
        sky,
    Should we false witness 'gainst our
        neighbour bear,   170
    Lest false and true in common ruin lie.
  Nor should fierce wrath of passion us
        ensnare
    To shed another's blood, and so to mar
    That face of God which we, His
        creatures, share.
IX. Nor will he from a deadly sin be far   175
    Who shall his neighbour's wife or goods
        desire,
    For then his base desires love's entrance
        bar.
X. The last of all is that our wills aspire
    No more to gain what is another's right,
    For that too parts us from our heavenly
        Sire.   180

Tenth into two separate precepts was needed, after the amalgamation of the First and Second, to keep up the numerical idea of the Decalogue.

And that we may be ready, day and night,
To keep His holy Law continually,
Vice shun we, for it sweeps us from His sight.

SEPTEM PECCATA MORTALIA

I. In Pride the root of every sin doth lie;
Hence man himself doth hold in loftier fame 185
Than others, and deserving lot more high.

II. Envy is that which makes us blush for shame,
With grief beholding others' happiness,
Like him whom we the foe of God proclaim.

III. Wrath still more woe doth on the wrathful press, 190
For its fierce mood lights up Hell's fiery heat;
Then ill deeds come, and loss of holiness.

IV. Sloth looks with hate on every action meet,
And to ill-doing ever turns the will,
Is slow to work, and quick to make retreat. 195

V. Then Avarice comes, through which the whole world still
Vexes its soul, and breaks through every law
And tempts with gain to every deed of ill.

184 The list of the seven deadly sins has at least the interest of

vi. Both fool and wise foul Gluttony doth
draw,
And he who pampers still his appetite, 200
Shortens his life, to fill his greedy maw.

vii. And Lust that comes the seventh in order
right,
The bonds of friendship breaks and
brotherhood,
At variance still with Truth and
Reason's light.

Let us against these sins have fortitude, 205
(They need but little ink to register)
So may we pass where loftiest pleasures
brood.

I say, to enter in that cloister fair,
Behoves we lift our orisons to God,
Whereof is first our Paternoster prayer. 210

PATERNOSTER

i. Our Father, who in Heaven hast Thine
abode,

ii. Thy name be ever hallowed in our
praise,
And thanks for all Thy goodness hath
bestowed.

presenting a parallel to the *Seven P.'s* of *Purg.* ix. 112. We may compare Chaucer's *Persone's Tale* as dealing more fully with the same subject.

211 Here we have an opportunity of comparing the real with the apocryphal Dante. A comparison of this Paraphrase of the *Paternoster* with that of *Purg.* xi. 1–21 will, I believe, enable us to measure the difference between the two. Here again one thinks that if the apocryphal story had been true, it would have been more effective to quote what had already appeared in the *Commedia*. It is suggestive that we find the same explanation of the *Libera nos a malo*.

III. Thy kingdom come, e'en as its meaning
weighs
IV. This prayer of ours, and may Thy will
prevail 215
V. On earth, as it in Heaven is done
always.
VI. Give, Father, of our bread the daily tale,
And may our sins be of Thy grace
forgiven,
Nor aught we do of Thy good pleasure
fail.
VII. And as we too forgive, do Thou from
Heaven 220
Grant, for Thy part, forgiveness full
and free,
To save us from the foes with whom
we've striven.
VIII. Our God and Father, Fount of Charity,
Protect and save us from the subtle
snare
Of Satan and his darts that deadly be; 225
So that to Thee we may uplift our prayer
That we Thy grace may merit, and
may come
Thy kingdom by devotion full to share.
IX. We pray Thee, Lord, whose glory lights
our gloom,
Guard us from troubles. Lo! to Thee
our heart 230
With lowly glance looks upward to its
Home.
The blessed Virgin-mother too has part,
And rightly, in our praises; well may
prove
Fit close for this, the service of our art.

We pray her that to grace of God's great
love 235
She lead us, by the might of her blest
prayer,
And from the snares of Hell our souls
remove.
And all who, through their sins in darkness fare
May she relume, and loose with gracious
mien
Unbinding from the toils of Hell's
despair. 240

AVE MARIA

Ave Maria, Mother, Maid, and Queen
Most Gracious, God doth ever with thee
stay;
Above all women high in heaven serene!
Blest also be thy Son, to whom I pray,
Our Jesus Christ, to guard us from all
ill, 245
And lead us with Him to eternal day.
Blest Virgin, may it ever be thy will
To let thy prayer to God for us arise,
That He may here be our Protector
still,
And bring us at the last to Paradise. 250

CANZONIERE

ECLOGUES

I

JOANNES DE VIRGILIO TO DANTE ALIGHIERI

Ah, gentle voice, to all the Muses dear,
Who with new rhymes dost soothe the troubled
 world,
Still striving, with the branch of life's true tree,
To cleanse it from the taint that bringeth
 death,

I

JOANNES DE VIRGILIO TO DANTE ALIGHIERI

There is to me something singularly touching in the poetical correspondence which now meets us. It belongs to the last years of Dante's life. The *Inferno* and *Purgatorio* were already finished when it began, and in some sense published. Before it closed the *Paradiso* also was completed, and *Ecl.* iv. contains, therefore, the last words that are extant from the poet's hand. It did not reach the friend to whom it was addressed till that hand was cold in death. After the manner of the style which they had chosen, the scholar records in his epitaph to the memory of the master that death had interrupted him in this return to the lighter and more graceful forms of Latin scholarship.

"*Pascua Pieriis demum resonabat avenis:*
Atropos heu! lectum livida rupit opus."

And the poems throw light on the occupations of the later years of Dante's life. The great work to which heaven and earth had lent their hands is finished, and there is no other work to take its place. What more natural than that the worn and weary spirit—worn and weary, and yet calmer and brighter than when he began the *Commedia*—should fall back upon the forms of composition in which he had gained his first laurels, and attained his first consciousness of the excellence of the "*bello stile*" (*H.* i. 87) which had won men's praise. That return to the classical studies of their boyhood has been familiar enough to us in the lives of English statesmen and men of letters. Fox and Lord Wellesley, and Lord Derby and Mr. Gladstone and Lord Stratford de Redcliffe, may serve by way of sample for a more complete induction.

One wishes that we had more information as to the young scholar

By laying bare to view the threefold coasts, 5
Assigned to souls, as merits may demand:
Hell for the lost; for those that seek the stars
Lethe; and realms above the sun for saints;

who was thus honoured by the poet's friendship. The epithet *Magister*, applied to him by Boccaccio and an anonymous commentator of the 14th century (Frat. *O. M.* i. 407), implies that he was recognised as, in some sense, a teacher or professor. The poems themselves show that he wrote from Bologna. It may perhaps be reasonably inferred from the fact that the title *de Virgilio* took the place of a patronymic that he did not belong to the class that piqued itself upon a descent from the older noble families of Italy. That name, however, obviously tells us more than this. It implies that he too had found in Virgil, as Dante, his master and his guide. As the Church historian of Cæsarea chose to call himself Eusebius Pamphili, that he might thus acknowledge his obligations to his early friend and instructor; as Peter Damian took his second name from the brother whom he loved (*Par.* xxi. 106, *n.*), so Giovanni identified himself by the new name, which thus indicated the poet whom he delighted to honour; and this, we may well believe, was the starting-point of Dante's regard for him. He addresses his friend as *senex*, and we may infer therefore that he was considerably the younger of the two. We can well understand, remembering how a difference of feeling as to the transcending merits of Virgil's genius had divided Dante from the *primo amico* of his own youth, Guido de' Cavalcanti (*H.* x. 52, *n.*), the joy with which he would welcome the affection of the young scholar, who, in this matter, was altogether like-minded with himself. Of the other facts recorded of the younger of the two, we may note that he is said to have taught Virgil, Statius, Lucan, Ovid, the four poets of *H.* iv., in a state-supported school at Bologna up to 1321, and to have removed afterwards to Cesena, where he probably died, and that he carried on a literary correspondence, of the same type as that on which we now enter, with the poet Albertino Musatto of Padua. Altogether I see in him one of the most noteworthy representatives of the earlier Italian renaissance. *Ecl.* i. 13 fixes the opening of the correspondence at a date subsequent to 1318. It is noticeable too, as Giovanni himself boasts in a poem to Musatto after Dante's death, that this was, as far as he knew (the Eclogues of Calpurnius were not discovered till the 15th century), the first revival of the Virgilian type.

"*Fistula non posthac nostris inflata poetis,*
Donec ea mecum certaret Tityrus olim
Lydius, Adriaco qui nunc in litore dormit,
Quà pineta sacras prætexunt saltibus umbras."

"That reed our later bards have left untouched
Till Tityrus, in days now past, with me
Competed,—Lydian Tityrus, who now
Sleeps on the Adrian shore, where pine-woods spread
Their sacred shadows on the grassy mead."

Why wilt thou still such lofty topics treat
For the rude herd, while we, with study pale, 10
Read nothing from thee, poet though thou art?
Sooner the wary dolphin with his lyre
Shall Davus guide, or solve the riddling Sphinx
Her knotty problems, than the headlong herd
Illiterate figure Tartarean depths, 15
And secrets of the Heaven, by Plato's self
Scarce fathomed; yet these things the town
 buffoon,
Who would drive Horace from the world,
 croaks out,

ECLOGUE I

1 It will be noted that *Ecl.* i. is simply an epistle in Latin verse. The bucolic form, with its Tityrus and Mopsus, is, characteristically enough, introduced by Dante in *Ecl.* ii. The opening lines show that the writer knew at least the scope and plan of the *Commedia*, as i. 25 indicates a special acquaintance with the Statius episode in *Purg.* xxi. 86–136. Joannes had probably been allowed to see the MS. of the first two cantiques. "Lethe" implies a knowledge of *Purg.* xxx. 143. The "bough" has been identified with the "laurel" of the poet, or the "wood" of *Exod.* xv. 25. More probably the writer alludes to the "golden branch" which served Æneas as a passport through the unseen world (*Æn.* vi. 143).

8 The scholar remonstrates with the master on the form which he had chosen. Why treat of such grave themes in the vulgar tongue and for the common people? We may infer that Dante's apology for his beloved *volgare* in *V. E.* i. 16, *Conv.* i. 6–13, had not come under his young friend's eyes. Davus (as in the "*Davus sum, non Œdipus*" of Terence, *Andr.* i. 2) is the typical man of no culture. Sooner might we think of him as equally able with Œdipus to solve the riddle of the Sphinx as to imagine him entering into the mysteries, beyond Plato's ken, of Purgatory and Paradise. Surely those who had grown pale with study had a claim on the poet they honoured.

17 Was the buffoon reciter to bawl out in the street the things he could not understand? If the words are taken as describing what had actually happened, they imply something like a general publication of the *Commedia*. Probably, however, they are only an anticipation of what may be, and the scholar appeals to the irritable sensitiveness which his friend had shown when, as in the stories told by (*Nov.* 114, 115) Sacchetti and others, he heard his earlier Italian poems mangled by blacksmiths and donkey-drivers as they pursued their calling.

By reason undigested. Thou wilt say,
"Not to these speak I, but to expert souls, 20
Though in the people's language." Well, the world
Of scholars scorns that language, were it one
Unvarying, not in thousand dialects.
And none of those with whom thou rank'st as sixth,
Nor he thou followest on thy heavenward path, 25
Wrote in the speech that through the market rings.
Wherefore, out-spoken critic of our bards,
If thou wilt give free course I'll speak my mind.
Be not too wasteful, throwing pearls to swine,
Nor clothe the sisterhood of Castaly 30
In unmeet raiment, but, I pray thee, choose
The speech that will most widely give thee fame
For thy prophetic song, the common lot
Of this and of that nation. Even now
Full many a theme there is that waits thy speech. 35

19 Dante might answer that he wrote not for the common herd, but for the men of culture. "Well," is the reply, "men of culture won't have the 'vulgar tongue' at any price." That would be true even if there was a recognised Italian language; how much more when there were only a thousand dialects?

24 Why not follow the five great Latin poets with whom Dante had joined himself in *H.* iv. 102, or Statius, whom he had met in *Purg.* xxi. 83-99? We are tempted to ask whether Joannes thought that they had written in a language "not understanded of the people" among whom they lived?

27 The words might refer to the criticisms in the *V. E.*, but, as we have seen reason to believe that the writer had not read that book, we may more probably connect them with passages like *Purg.* xxiv. 55-63, xxvi. 97-126, which he had just been reading.

35 Yes, a Latin poem would give Dante a wider fame, not limited to his own nation; and as for subjects, the scholar can suggest a round half-dozen for his master's choice. There was the Italian campaign of Henry VII., the war of Uguccione della

Tell with what flight the bearer of Jove's bolts
Made for the stars: tell what the flowerets fair
And what the lilies that the plowman crushed:
Tell of the Phrygian does that wounded lie,
Torn by the teeth of fierce Molossian hounds; 40
Tell of Ligurian mountains, and the fleets
Of fair Parthenope, in verse of thine,
So that thy fame may spread to Gades old,
Alcides' city, and that Ister's stream
May hear and wonder, as will Pharos too, 45
And where Elissa once was owned as queen.
If fame delight thee, it will scarce content
To be cooped up within a narrower sphere,
And find thy glory in the vile herd's praise.
Lo I, the priest—if thou that claim concede— 50
Of those fair nymphs who haunt Aonian hills,
And Maro's servant, bearing Virgil's name,
Will gladly be the first to lead thee forth,
'Mid crowds of loud-applauding worshippers,
Thy temples crowned with wreaths of fragrant
bays, 55
E'en as the herald, mounted on his horse,

Faggiuola (*Ball.* xv.) against the "lilies" of the city of flowers, or that of Can Grande, the Molossian mastiff, against the Paduans (1312), who, as claiming descent from Antenor, are described as Phrygians, or that of Robert II. of Naples against Piedmont and Genoa. A poem on such subjects as these might win a widespread fame, for which the *Commedia* could never hope, from east and west, and north and south. "Pharos," of course, points to Alexandria, and "Elissa" is Dido. What a field was open to ambition there! What an example, we add, of the irony of history we might have had, had the master followed the scholar's counsels!

50 The ambition of the scholar led him to picture to himself his own share in the triumph. Would it not be a proud moment for Dante as well as for himself to crown him in the school of Bologna with the poet's wreath? What he had said as to subjects for an epic was not enough. There was yet a wider choice. Mountains and seas were alike full of wars and rumours of war, only waiting for the touch of the poet's hand, and without that, destined to be left unsung. He hints even that his friend's song might restrain the fierce passions of the combatants.

Exults, proclaiming loud with echoing voice
His leader's trophies to the joyful crowd.
E'en now the alarm of war affrights mine ears:
What threats are those of father Apennine? 60
Why are Tyrrhenian waves by Nereus lashed?
Why rages Mars on this side or on that?
Take thou thy lyre, and calm that tumult wild.
Unless thou sing of this, while other bards
Hang on thee, that alone thou sing to all, 65
They will remain untold. Yet even now,
If thou, who dwell'st hard by Eridanus,
Give me the hope that thou wilt visit me,
And count me worthy of some kindly lines,
And if it irk thee not to read my verse, 70
Weak though it be—e'en such as goose o'er-
bold
Might cackle to the swan of sweetest song—
Or answer, Master mine, or grant my prayer.

67 As sojourning in Ravenna, communicating with one of the mouths of the Po by a canal, Dante was described as a dweller by that river. He had given his friend the hope that he would some day or other visit him at Bologna, and show that he counted him worthy of his friendship. To that visit Joannes looked forward. Meanwhile the swan of Italian poetry will perhaps condescend to listen even to the cackling of the goose. One feels, however, as one reads that last line, that the young poet looked on himself as at least an ugly duckling growing towards swanhood.

II

DANTE ALIGHIERI TO JOANNES DE VIRGILIO

THOSE letters black on patient paper traced
We read, those warblings from Pierian breast,
Flowing so softly, flowing too for us.
And so it chanced we told our tale of goats
Fresh from their pastures, I beneath the oak, 5
And Melibœus with me. He indeed—
For much he sought with me to read that
song—
"O Tityrus," began, "I pray thee tell
What Mopsus means?" And I, O Mopsus,
smiled.
And then he urged his question more and
more. 10

ECLOGUE II

We can imagine the half-amused feeling with which the master read the scholar's letter. In adopting as the form of his answer the pattern presented by the Virgilian Eclogues, there is perhaps a playful reminder that he too knows something of Virgil; that he is as skilled in that "*bello stilo*" as the young poet who assumed the cognomen of "*de Virgilio.*" Yes, he will be Tityrus, the "*fortunatus senex*" of *Ecl.* i. 47. And the Melibœus who is with him is (so the early commentators tell us) the Dino Perini of Florence, the poet's friend, whose name has met us in the story of the first seven cantos of the *Inferno.* In designating Joannes as Mopsus there is possibly a sportive reference to *Ecl.* v. 2—

"*Boni quoniam convenimus ambo,*
Tu calamos inflare leves, ego dicere versus."

It was well that the younger bard should be reminded of the nature and limits of his gift.

[4] The two friends are together when the letter comes. Perini waits to know its contents. Dante smiles instead of answering (comp. *V. N.* c. 4). The goatherd had better look after his goats (*Purg.* xxvii. 86), *i.e.*, his scholars.

Conquered at last by my great love for him,
My laughter scarce repressed, I answered him.
"Why ravest thou, O foolish one?" said I,
"The goats thou tendest, they demand thy
care,
E'en though thy meagre fare may vex thee too. 15
Unknown to thee the pastures where the shade
Of Mænalus o'erhangs, and hides the sun
With sloping summit—pastures decked in tints
Of thousand hues of grasses and of flowers.
A lowly stream, by willow boughs o'erhung, 20
Surrounds them, from its surface scattering dew
O'er all its banks, and hollows out a way
Where waters wander at their own sweet will,
From the high summit flowing. Mopsus there,
While o'er the pliant grass his oxen rove, 25
Contemplates, at his ease, of men and gods
The labours. Then, through pipes that swell
with wind,
He to his inner joys gives utterance,
So that his sweet songs draw his herds to him,
And lions calmed rush from the mountain's
height 30
Down to the plain, and waters stay their course
And mountain height and forest nod their
heads."
"O Tityrus," spake he, "if Mopsus sings
In unknown pastures, yet his unknown songs

17 Mænalus, the mountain of Arcadia, stands for the bucolic poetry in which Dante claims to be an expert. It "conceals the sun," because it interposes the veil of allegory between the reader and its true meaning. The description of the stream which flows from the mountain reminds us of Dante's account of his own special excellence as a poet in *Purg.* xxiv. 52–54. The description of Mopsus as a second Orpheus is obviously not without a touch of playful irony.

33 Meliboeus presses his inquiries. It might be well for his scholars to learn the Virgilian verses which Mopsus had jus sent

I yet may teach to these my wandering goats 35
With thee to guide me." What then could I do,
When he thus urged me, panting eagerly?
"O Meliboeus, to Aonian hills
Mopsus has given himself, year following year,
While others toil o'er law and equity, 40
And in the holy mountain's shade grows pale,
Washed in the stream that quickens poets' life,
And full, till breast, throat, palate overflow
With milk of song; my Mopsus summons me
To take the leaves that grow on Peneus' shore, 45
Where Daphne was transformed."
"What wilt thou do?"
Said Meliboeus. "Wilt thou ever keep
Thy brows undecked with laurels, through the fields
As shepherd known?" "Nay, name and fame of seer, 50
Oft vanish, Meliboeus, into air,
And scarcely has the Muse our Mopsus brought
To full completeness, spite of sleepless nights."
Then spake I, indignation finding voice:

to his master. Tityrus can no longer refuse to answer his questions. "Mopsus is a votary of the Muses, dwelling on the Aonian Mount. He summons me to put in my claim to the laureate wreath." The daughter of Peneus is Daphne, loved by Apollo, and transformed into a laurel (*Met.* i. 452–567).

47 "Well," is Meliboeus Perini's natural question, "will you act on that suggestion, write a poem, submit it to the judgment of scholars, and claim the laurel?"

50 The poet's answer is twofold. He has fallen on evil days, and scarcely even Mopsus, with all his restless study, has gained the reputation of a poet. But great as might be the honour of the laureate wreath, Bologna does not attract him. The Guelph anti-imperial city is no place for him. Rather will he wait till he can return to Florence (*Par.* xxv. 1–12), and claim it there. The "*flavescere*" of the original in l. 62 points to a less swarthy complexion than that which we commonly associate with Dante's name, and so far agrees with the Bargello portrait.

"What echoes will from hills and fields
resound, 55
If with a laurelled brow I tune my lyre
To pæan hymns? And yet I own I fear
The thickets wild, and fields that know not
God.
Were it not better done to deck my locks
With triumph-wreath, and should I e'er return 60
Where my own Arno flows, to hide them there,
Now grey, once golden, 'neath the laurel
crown?"
And he, "Who doubts this? Yet, O Tityrus,
Bethink thee, therefore, how the time flies fast,
The she-goats are grown old whom once we
paired, 65
That they might bring forth young."
Then I replied,
"When in my song the sea-girt mountain high,
And those who dwell within the starry spheres,
Shall be revealed, as now the realms of Hell, 70
Then 'twill be well with ivy and with bay
To crown my brows. Will Mopsus grant me
this?"
"Mopsus!" he answered, "See'st thou not
that he
Condemns the speech of that thy Comedy,

63 Meliboeus reminds his friend that time passes quickly. The young scholars who would welcome his poem are growing up into manhood.

67 "Yes," is the poet's answer; "when I have finished my *Purgatory* and my *Paradise*, then, and resting my claims on them, the poet's wreath will be welcome." Mopsus, perhaps, will allow that. This leads to the question what Mopsus had said, and then to this Dante replies that he, Mopsus, contemns that form of poetry in the vulgar tongue which even women can read and recite, and he reads the *Eclogue* which he had received. Meliboeus naturally asks how they shall convert Mopsus to a better mind. And the answer is not far to seek. In bucolic language Dante has an ewe-goat from whose udders the milk flows freely and without constraint.

As by the lips of women trite and worn, 75
Rejected by the nymphs of Castaly?"
"So is it," I replied, and then again
I read thy verses, Mopsus. With a shrug
He answered, "What then lies within our reach
Our Mopsus to convert?" And then I said, 80
"I have an ewe, thou know'st her goodliest far
Of all the flock, in milk abounding so
That scarce she bears the weight of udders
full,—
'Neath the vast rock just now she chews the
cud,—
Joined to no flock, accustomed to no fold. 85
Of her free will, unforced, she never fails
To seek the milk-pail. Her 'tis in my mind
To milk with ready hands, and ten jugs full
Will I to Mopsus send." "Do thou meanwhile
Watch all the frolics of the gamesome goats, 90
And learn to fix thy teeth in hardest crusts."
So sang we then beneath our oak boughs, I
And Melibœus, while our poor abode
Saw homely meal preparing on the hearth.

He will send him ten pails of that milk, that he may taste and judge. In other words he will let him see ten Cantos of the *Paradiso*.

89-91 I assign these words to Melibœus. He warns Dante to beware of the men whom he has held up to reproof in the *Commedia*, and has thus made his enemies, and of the hardships (*Par.* xvii. 116-120) which result from that enmity.

III

JOANNES DE VIRGILIO TO DANTE ALIGHIERI

Beneath the hills well watered, where we see
Savena meet with Reno, sportive nymph,
Her snowy locks entwined with wreaths of
green,
I found a shelter in a rock-hewn cave.
My heifers cropped the herbage on the banks, 5
Lambs browsed on tender grass, the goats on
shrubs.
What should I do? for I alone was there
As dweller in the woods, the rest being gone
Full speed into the city, business-pressed;
No Nysa or Alexis answered me, 10
Before, such constant comrades. With my hook
I carved me pipes of water-reeds;—best cure
Is that for hours that linger—when the shade
Of Adrian shore, there where the crowded pines
In their long rows and stretching up to heaven, 15
O'erhang the fields as guardian deities,

ECLOGUE III

1 The Sarpina (Savena) and Reno are the two rivers of Bologna. The former divides into two branches, known as the Old and the New, to which the epithets "green" and "snowy" respectively refer. Adopting the bucolic style of his master, Joannes describes himself as in solitude while his scholars had left him for their business in the city, and he was tuning his flageolet, *i.e.*, taking up his pen to write, when he heard the pipe of Tityrus resounding on the Adrian shore. In other words, he has received Dante's *Eclogue* and the ten Cantos which accompanied it. The former he admires. It is long since the poets of Italy had heard anything like it. It charms not only Virgilian scholars like himself, but even men of rougher moods and lower culture. It stirs him up to imitation. He too will play on the Virgilian reed, and for a time lay aside his graver tasks. Benacus (= Lago di Garda), from which the Mincio flows to Mantua, represents the birthplace of Virgil.

Fields sweet with myrtles and with thousand flowers,
And where the watery Ram leaves no sands dry,
But craves for showers his soft fleece to bedew—
The whistling wind of Eurus blowing soft, 20
Brought to my ears the song of Tityrus,
Borne on the vocal fragrance, o'er the heights
Of Mænalus, balm-breathing on the ear,
And in the mouth milk-dropping, like to which
For many a day the guardians of the flock 25
Remember not, though all Arcadians be.
Arcadian nymphs rejoice to hear the song,
Shepherds, and sheep, and shaggy goats, and kine;
E'en the wild asses run with pricked-up ears,
And fauns come dancing from Lyceian heights. 30
And to myself I said, "If Tityrus
Thus charm the sheep, the cattle, and the goats
Whilst thou, a dweller in the town, didst sing
The song of cities, how long is it since
The reed, Benacus-grown, has touched thy lips 35
In shepherd's song? Nay, let him hear that thou,
Thou too a shepherd, singest in the woods."
Nor did I linger then, but laid aside
The greater reeds, and seized the slender ones,
To breathe a new strain with my labouring lips. 40

31 Characteristically the scholar thinks more of the *Eclogue* than of the *Paradiso*. If the "divine old man" would but write always like this, he would be a second Virgil—Virgil himself reappearing on earth, as in the Pythagorean doctrine of transmigration. His friends Mopsus and Meliboeus may now follow—the latter, indeed, had already followed—his example.

36 Tityrus, in the bitterness of his life as an exile, might rightly pour out the vials of his wrath on Florence, but he might spare the

And so, divine old man, thou wilt be found
A second Tityrus; nay, the very man,—
If we give credit to the Samian. So
Let Mopsus speak as Melibœus spoke.
Ah me! that thou shouldst dwell in squalid hut, 45
With dust o'erlaid, and shouldst in righteous wrath,
Mourn for the fields of Arno, fields from thee
Stolen, and from thy flocks. Ah, deed of shame
For that ungrateful city! Yet I pray
Wet not thy Mopsus' cheeks with flowing tears, 50
Nor in thy wrath torment thyself and him,
Whose love clings round thee full as close—I say,
As close, O good old man, as doth the vine,
That with a hundred tendrils clasps the elm.
Oh, that once more thou mightest see thy locks, 55
Locks grey and sacred, gain a second youth,
Grown golden, and be trimmed by Phyllis' self.
How wilt thou then behold with wondering look

scholar who loved him and clung round him as the vine clings round the elm.

44 Ah! if he could but return to Florence and revisit his home once again! Is Phyllis, we ask, the Gemma, of whom we hear so little? Did Joannes know that it was *the* grief of Dante's life to have been parted from her? (*Par.* xvii. 55). But meanwhile will he not visit him at Bologna and join him in his studies? Each poet might write according to his age. He describes his home and the hospitality which he offers in glowing colours, but, of course, after the bucolic fashion. The "wild thyme" perhaps stands for philosophic studies; "poppy" for the soothing influences of the medical studies in which Dante found refreshment. We note, at all events, a reference to the sleeplessness from which Dante apparently suffered. The mushroom and pepper, the garlic, the honey and the apples, stand, we may suppose, for different forms of literature, the words

Thy vine-clad cottage! Yet, lest long delay
Bring weariness, thou may'st awhile rejoice 60
To see my joy, the caves where I find rest;
Refresh thyself with me. We both will sing;
I, with my slender reed, thou playing still
The part of master, with more majesty,
So that age find his fitting place for each. 65
The place itself invites thee, flowing stream
Purls through the cavern which the rocks
protect,
And where the shrubs waft breezes; and
around
Wild marjoram pours its fragrance, and for
sleep
The poppy grows, and brings—so men report— 70
A sweet forgetfulness; a couch for thee
Of wilding thyme shall our Alexis strew
Whom Corydon bids me call, and willingly
Will Nysa gird herself to wash thy feet,
And get thy supper ready. Thestylis 75
Shall season mushrooms with the pungent dust
Of pepper, and subdue the garlic strong,
If Melibœus chance to gather that,
Too rashly, in his garden. Hum of bees
Shall bid thee to eat honey. Apples sweet 80

of the wise, the satires, the sonnets, the *canzoni* which made up a poet's feast.

85 65 And all honour will be paid to the visitor. Ivy is there for the poet's wreath. The students of Bologna (Parrhasius, as an Arcadian mountain, is the symbol of culture), and they will rejoice in the new poems (*qu.* the *Eclogue*?) and the old (*qu.* the *Commedia*?). They will bring their tributes of honour (*qu.* panegyric verses?), such as Melibœus-Perini had delighted in when he received them at Bologna.

9?, 77 And why should Tityrus fear Bologna? Men of high and low estate are ready to give pledges of their faithfulness. He might, at least, visit the scholar to whom he was so dear. Chiron and Apollo had not disdained the shepherd's life in a strange land, and why should he?

105 80 Then a new thought occurs to him, and Mopsus makes answer

Shall be for thee to gather and to taste,
Rosy as Nysa's cheeks are; much beside
Thou wilt not touch as being all too fair;
And o'er the cave the ivy creeps and creeps.
With wreaths prepared for thee. And, in a word, 85
No pleasure shall be lacking. Come thou then,
And with thee come all those who wish to see
Thy presence with us, young and old alike,
From hills Parrhasian, all who would admire
In joy thy newer songs, and learn the old. 90
These will to thee their offerings bring, or goats,
Fresh from the woods, or spotted hides of lynx,
As Melibœus once was wont to do.
Come then, and fear not, Tityrus, our fields:
The lofty pines with waving heads give pledge 95
Of safety for thee; even so the shrubs,
And acorn-bearing oaks. No wiles are here,
No plots, as thou dost deem, of frauds and wrong,
Wilt thou not trust thyself to me who love thee?
Perchance thou scornest this my poor abode: 100
And yet the gods have not disdained to dwell
In hollow caverns, witness Chiron old,

to himself. Iolas (Virg. *Ecl.* iv. 57, makes him the rich lover of Alexis), *i.e.*, Guido da Polenta of Ravenna, Dante's host and patron, will not allow him to leave, and Dante himself will prefer Ravenna to Bologna. Why should the scholar thus seek after the unattainable? Well, he can only plead that he follows the law of his nature. He admires, and therefore he must love.

114- In the absence of Tityrus, Mopsus will console himself with Muso, *sc.* with Musatto, a Latin poet of Padua of some eminence. Dante, who "drank of the waters of the Arno," *i.e.*, wrote Italian poetry, and cared little for the Latin verses of his contemporaries,

Achilles' foster-father, and Apollo,
Who lived a shepherd with the sons of men.
"Art thou mad, Mopsus? Nay, Iolas, he, 105
The man of polished culture, will refuse,
Seeing that thy gifts are but a peasant's store,
Nor is thy cave as safe as are the tents
Where Tityrus seeks repose. But what desire,
So eager, leads thee, what new impulse stirs 110
Thy feet?" The maid still gazes on the
youth,
The youth on bird, the bird upon the woods,
Mopsus on thee, O Tityrus, and that gaze
Engenders love. Reject me then, and I
Will quench my thirst with Muso, Phrygian-
born. 115
Truly thou know'st this not; thou drinkest
still
Of thine own country's waters.
Why then, why
Hear I my heifers lowing? Why flow streams
Fourfold of milk between the dropping thighs? 120
I have it: I will haste to fill the pails
With fresh warm milk wherein the hardest
crusts
Shall pass to softness. Come then to the pail,
We'll send as many jugs to Tityrus
As he has promised us. And yet, perchance, 125
'Tis a bold thing to offer milk to one
Himself a shepherd.
Even while I speak
My friends draw near, and on the mountain
height
The setting sun sinks down behind the ridge.

was perhaps ignorant of his fame. Lastly, he ends by sending ten poems of his own in return for those which he had received.

IV

DANTE ALIGHIERI TO JOANNES DE VIRGILIO

Eôus, with the Colchian fleece bedecked,
And all the other wingèd steeds were bearing,
With headlong course, the Titan wondrous fair.
His orbit, where it just begins to slope
From its mid-height, held each wheel of the
car 5
In even balance, and the glittering rays,
By shadows oft o'ercome, now, in their turn,
O'ercame the shadows, and the fields grew hot.
And therefore, in their pity for their flocks,
Alphesibœus, yea, and Tityrus, 10
Fled to the woods, the woods wherein the ash,
Together with the plane and linden, grows,
And while the sheep that wander in the fields,
Goats mingled with them, lie upon the grass,
And sniff the breeze, lo! Tityrus reclined, 15
Now full of years, beneath a maple's shade,

ECLOGUE IV

1 The opening lines remind us of *Purg.* ix. 1-9, both being based upon *Met.* ii. 1-30. Eôus (= the Dawn) was the name of one of the horses of the sun (*Met.* ii. 153). The epithet "Colchian" points, with its allusions to the golden fleece, to the spring-tide when the sun was in *Aries* (*H.* i. 38). It was noon and the sun was hot.

7 The new interlocutor Alphesibœus, is identified by commentators with Fiducio de' Milotti of Certaldo (Boccaccio's birthplace), a physician of high repute, then staying at Ravenna.

16 The subjects of which Alphesibœus spoke were naturally enough partly physical, partly metaphysical, such as two students of science might discuss together. Of some of them we find traces in Dante's other writings; as, *e.g.*, of the return of souls to the stars under whose influence they had been born, from which, in one form of Platonism, they were believed to have come (*Par.* iv. 52). The other questions turn mainly on the zoology of the time, such as suited the studies of the physician.

By the soft, slumbrous fragrance sleep-
oppressed,
While on his thick-knobbed staff, from pear-
tree torn,
Alphesibœus leant, that he might speak.
And then he said, "That souls of men
ascend 20
Up to those stars whence they came down to us,
Within our bodies a new home to find;
That snow-white swans make all Caÿster's
banks
Re-echo with their songs, in mildest clime
Rejoicing, and the marshes of the vale;— 25
That the dumb fishes leave the deeper sea
In shoals, where rivers first approach the
bounds
Of Nereus;—that Hyrcanian tigers stain,
With crimson gore, the heights of Caucasus;
That Libyan serpent with its scaly tail 30
Makes furrows in the sand:—at all this I
Have ceased to wonder; for to all that live
Appropriate environment brings joy;
But Mopsus moves my wonder, moves it too

[25] In all these instances there were the workings of the law of "like to like," or at least of the choice of a suitable environment. What Alphesibœus could not understand was that Mopsus should be content to remain in such a Cyclops' den as Bologna. The personal Cyclops is identified with Romeo de' Pepoli, then ruler of that city, under whose protection Joannes lived. Romeo is reported to have been a Ghibelline (*Vill.* ix. 132; Troja, *Veltro*, pp. 179–180), but Dante apparently had personal reasons for distrusting him.

[28] At this point Melibœus-Perini arrives, panting in hot haste as the bearer of the last Eclogue from Joannes. The older scholars smile as when the Sicilians saw Sergestus torn from the rock to which he clung when his boat foundered (*Æn.* v. 200–283).

[30] Tityrus raises his head and asks the reason of the breathless haste. Then, as with a taste for a marvel after the manner of Ovid, lo! of its own accord—for Melibœus is too much out of breath to play on it—the reed breathes forth the first line of the Eclogue which the scholar had sent to his master. The hundred verses stand for the actual ninety-seven of the Eclogue.

In all the shepherds that with me abide 35
In fair Sicilian fields, that he prefers
Where Ætna smokes, the Cyclops' cave and
rocks."
So spake he. Then all hot with panting
breath
Comes Melibœus: scarce had he exclaimed
"O Tityrus!" when all the elders mocked 40
His youthful, high-pitched voice, as once of
yore
Sicanians mocked when they Sergestus saw
Snatched from the rock. And then the old
man raised
His grey hairs from the grass, and to the youth,
Whose nostrils still were panting, thus began: 45
"Ah friend o'er-young, what fresh-born care
is this,
That makes thee vex thy lungs with pace so
quick?"
He nothing answered, but his lips then
touched,
His trembling lips, the pipe of oaten straw,
And thence no single note fell on the ear, 50
But, as the youth was striving to draw out
Tones from his reed, the reed itself breathes
forth—

67 Pelorus stands for Ravenna, as the true Sicily, the true home of shepherds and their poets.

71 The king is Midas, who asked and obtained the power of turning whatever he touched into gold. When Bromius (= Bacchus) taught him that he might free himself from the power which had become a bondage by bathing in the Pactolus, the reeds whispered the fact that the king had ass's ears (*Met.* xi. 143-146). That spontaneous utterance found, so Alphesibœus thought, a parallel in the Eclogue-song that had flowed from the reed without human lips applied to it. He excuses himself for thinking that a marvel like that might have overcome Dante's hesitation. He urges that he should still refuse to trust himself. The Dryads of Ravenna and all his friends call on him to stay. They felt that he could not venture without risk to his life.

I speak a thing most wonderful yet true—
"Beneath the hills well watered, where we
see
Savena meet with Reno." Had he then 55
But thrice upon the mouth-piece blown, I
trow
That he with five-score songs had soothed
the ear
Of silent shepherds, and that Tityrus
Had listened, and with him Alphesibœus.
And him Alphesibœus thus addressed, 60
Our Tityrus, "Would'st thou, honoured old
man, dare
To leave Pelorum's dewy plains, and seek
The Cyclops' cavern?"
And he made reply:
"Why dost thou doubt? Why, dear friend,
question me?" 65
"Why do I doubt? Why question thee?"
then spake
Alphesibœus. "Hear'st thou not what sound
Comes from the flute in its melodious might,
God-given, like the reeds, the breeze-born
reeds,
As rumour spreads far off the change that
passed 70
O'er the king's temples, in their foul dis-
grace,
When he, as Bromios bade him, straightway
changed
Pactolus' sands to hue of glittering gold?
Since he calls thee to where the shore is
strewn
With Ætna's pumice dust, O blest old man, 75
Trust not delusive favour; look with pity

Upon the hallowed spot where Dryads haunt,
And on thy flocks. The mountain height, the
downs,
The streams, will weep, bereaved of thee : the
Nymphs,
Fearing worse things, will weep for thee with
me. 80
And the ill-will Pachynus bears to us,
Will all subside. And we too shall regret,
We shepherds, having known thee. Blest old
man,
Abandon not the pastures and the springs,
On which thy name hath stamped a deathless
life." 85
"O more, by merit more, than half this
heart,"
Touching his breast, spake aged Tityrus,
"Mopsus, in love bound up with me for
those
Who fled Pyreneus' passion wild of yore,
Because I dwell, the Po upon my right, 90
And on the left the Rubicon, where sea

81 Pachynus, the southern promontory of Sicily, stands probably for the kingdom of Naples, whose ruler, Robert II. (*Purg.* vii. 119; *Par.* xix. 130, xx. 63) had shown himself one of Dante's bitterest enemies. His hostility would cease because it would be satisfied with what would be Dante's ruin. That ruin might even bring trouble on his friends.

85 The poet's consciousness that his name will live, and that without writing a Latin epic, reminds us of *H.* iv. 102; *Purg.* xi. 98; *Par.* xvii. 118–120.

88 Alphesibœus was a bosom friend, but Mopsus also, as a votary of the Muses, might claim some share in his affections. The lines allude to the story in *Met.* v. 287–331, that Pyreneus had invited the Muses to take shelter beneath his roof; that he then offered them violence; that they took their winged flight from the tower of his house, and that he threw himself after them and perished. Was this a gentle warning to Joannes not to claim too exclusive an intimacy with the Muses whom he loved?

90 Mopsus had written as though Dante were living (as, of course, he was literally) between the Po and the Rubicon, in the Æmilian region of Romagnuola, and sang the praises of his own Ætna (*i.e.*,

Of Adria bounds the fair Æmilian land,
Commends to us the pastures by the shore
Of Ætna, little knowing that we both
Dwell in the soft grass of Trinacrian height, 96
More fruitful far than all Sicilian hills
In food for flocks and herds. And yet, though rocks
Of Ætna fall far short of those green fields
Pelorum boasts, I fain would leave my flock,
And as thou wishest, come to visit thee, 100
My Mopsus, but for fear of Polypheme."
And then Alphesibœus made reply,
"Who fears not Polypheme, with human blood
Still wont to stain his lips, from that same hour
When Galatea saw her Acis' limbs, 105
Poor Acis! torn asunder! Scarcely she
Herself escaped. Would spell of love prevail
When his fierce rage was kindled to such heat?
And scarce could Achæmenides restrain
His soul from parting, when he looked and saw 110

Bologna), as though that were the home of poets. He was ignorant that Ravenna was the true Trinacria (=Sicily), the land where Theocritus would have loved to dwell. And his Pelorum was "green." It was the symbol of the national poetry, in the spoken language of the people, which Mopsus despised, but which was destined to be far more fertile than the Ætnæan region, the classical poetry, which he loved.

101 Polyphemus is, as before, Romeo de' Pepoli (l. 25). It was Dante's distrust of him that led him to decline his friend's invitation. The outrages named are those attributed to the literal Polyphemus (*Met.* xiii. 739–898). Possibly they refer to some recent acts of cruelty on Romeo's part.

109 Achæmenides was one of the companions of Ulysses, whom Æneas encountered in Sicily (*Æn.* iii. 590-681). Here also there may probably be an historical allusion now irrecoverably lost to us.

The Cyclops, with his comrades' blood
besprent.
Ah, thou, my bosom friend, I pray thee,
check
That fearful wish that Reno and the Nymph
Thou praisest, close, within their boundaries,
This honoured head, to gather wreaths for
which 115
Wreaths that fade not e'en now prepares
himself
The dresser of the vineyard."
Tityrus,
Smiling in concord with him, heart and
soul,
In silence listened to his scholar's words,
As by the whole flock spoken. But be-
cause 120
The horses of the chariot of the Sun
Were moving downwards through the ether
pure,
So that the shadows o'er all nature spread,
The shepherds, leaving valley cool, and
woods,

113 The Naiad is the nymph of the Savena joined with the Reno, as in *Ecl.* iii. 1. The "Virgin" is, of course, Daphne, transformed into a laurel (*Met.* i. 486).

The expectation that the laurel wreath was ready to be cut for him had an unlooked-for fulfilment. The Eclogue did not reach his scholar-friend till the hand that wrote it was cold in death, and the laurel wreath was placed upon his brow by Guido da Polenta.

117 Tityrus-Dante recognised that the words of Alphesibœus were those of the whole company of his friends. He therefore would abide by his decision, and would not go to Bologna.

121 The steeds are those of the sun-chariot, now hasting to its setting. The conversation was over, and the friends separated. Meanwhile Iolas (Guido da Polenta) had been listening, and he it was (the writer of the Eclogue seems now to distinguish between himself and the ideal Tityrus of the poem) who had reported the dialogue to Dante, as he did to his scholar at Bologna. In the original the last words of the last line *poimus* (as an equivalent for ποιοῦμεν) we have a noteworthy instance of Dante's boldness as

Followed their flocks that took their home-
ward way, 125
And shaggy goats went foremost, as they
took
Their path to soft green meadows ; and
meanwhile
Iolas crafty, listening stood hard by,
Who heard all this and told all this to us :
He sings to us, O Mopsus, we to thee. 130

the coiner of new words to meet his wants, a proof also that he had at least some knowledge of Greek.

INDEX OF FIRST LINES OF THE MINOR POEMS

(*Italian and Latin**)

* *Ball.*, Ballata; *Canz.*, Canzone; *Ecl.*, Eclogue; *Sest.*, Sestina; *Son.*, Sonetto; *St.*, Stanza.

INDEX OF FIRST LINES

INDEX OF FIRST LINES OF THE MINOR POEMS

(Translation)

NDEX OF FIRST LINES

INDEX OF FIRST LINES

INDEX OF SUBJECTS AND NAMES

INDEX OF SUBJECTS AND NAMES

INDEX OF SUBJECTS AND NAMES

ADVERTISEMENTS

CPSIA information can be obtained
at www.ICGtesting.com
Printed in the USA
LVHW081608150121
676573LV00007B/198

9 781346 375274